There Is No Place Like
Work

"*There Is No Place Like Work* guides leaders in successfully defining and managing their culture to build a dedicated workforce. It has applications in academic, professional and applied settings."

Deborah L. Levy, PhD,
Harvard Medical School

"A lot of amazing information packed into a few easy-to-read pages. No one can afford NOT to read this book."

Joel E. Marks, President,
Innovative Brokerage Solutions, Inc.

"These seasoned experts know what it takes to help you focus on success. Their keen insight is a gift to the business world!"

Robyn Freedman Spizman, Author,
The Giftionary

There Is No Place Like Work

Seven Leadership Insights for Creating a Workplace to Call Home

Sheila L. Margolis, PhD • Ava S. Wilensky, PhD

Gibbs Smith, Publisher
Salt Lake City

First Edition
10 09 08 07 06   5 4 3 2

Published by

Gibbs Smith, Publisher
PO Box 667
Layton, Utah 84041
Orders: 1.800.748.5439
www.gibbs-smith.com

Printed and bound in Michigan

Library of Congress Cataloging-in-Publication Data

Margolis, Sheila L.
There is no place like work : seven leadership insights for creating a work-place to call home / Sheila L. Margolis and Ava S. Wilensky.— 1st ed.
p. cm.
ISBN 1-58685-883-1
1. Quality of work life. 2. Corporate culture. I. Wilensky, Ava S. II. Title.

HD6955.M336 2006
658.3'12—dc22

2005027787

This book is dedicated to our husbands,

Mike Margolis and Bob Wilensky,

who have supported us in our search

for meaningful work.

CONTENTS

PART I
A Workplace to Call Home

PART II
Behind the Wizard's Curtain

FOREWORD

By Roger S. Baum

Great-grandson of L. Frank Baum, creator of *The Wonderful Wizard of Oz*

THERE Is No Place Like Work by Dr. Sheila L. Margolis and Dr. Ava S. Wilensky reminds us that business success, just like all success in life, comes primarily from within each of us. Like the characters in *The Wonderful Wizard of Oz*, we travel down our respective Yellow Brick Roads seeking answers. We, too, are often faced with challenges in our personal and business lives that sometimes seem insurmountable.

In *There Is No Place Like Work*, Drs. Margolis and Wilensky draw a parallel between the journey to Oz and the journey to a meaningful workplace. As you take this journey, you will learn how to analyze and manage your company's culture and create a workplace that fits who you are and what you want your company to be. The insights in *There Is No Place Like Work* give you a simply ingenious way to accomplish this goal. I don't believe anyone has ever presented the path to success so beautifully and clearly. I thank Drs. Margolis and Wilensky for putting this valuable journey in perspective.

The Wonderful Wizard of Oz has survived for more than one hundred years. Perhaps someday people will ask you, "How did your company survive after all these years?" I believe you will merely need to hand them a copy of this unique book.

I wish you a wonderful journey to your Reflection City.

My darling child! [Aunt Em] cried, folding
the little girl in her arms and covering her
face with kisses; *where in the world
did you come from?*

From the Land of Oz, said Dorothy, gravely.
*And here is Toto, too. And oh, Aunt Em!
I'm so glad to be at home again!*

L. Frank Baum,
The Wonderful Wizard of Oz

PREFACE

IMAGINE hearing your employees say, "This company is like family." "I can't imagine working any place else." "This is where I belong." Well, you don't have to travel over the rainbow to achieve that level of dedication and commitment from your employees. You can find the answers within your own company—by understanding your workplace culture. Contrary to popular belief, culture is not some amorphous and accidental phenomenon. This crucial element in long-range organizational success is definable, measurable and moldable. That process is called CORE Culture Management, and you will learn to master it by understanding CORE Culture and the Five Ps.

We wrote *There Is No Place Like Work* to explain how to analyze your CORE Culture, align it with your workplace practices and, as a leader, gain the insight necessary to shape it. The goal: to competitively express your organization's essential nature in a way that yields bottom-line success. This effort is not simply philosophical, although Philosophy is an element of it. This book is a practical tool for making more money, coping better with change and creating a genuinely dedicated workforce.

There Is No Place Like Work is based on hands-on, real-world concepts we have used with CEOs, managers and employees in organizations ranging from the Fortune 500 to nonprofit. These organizations have accomplished the ultimate goal of managing their CORE Culture: to build a staff of motivated employees who feel individually that they are doing meaningful tasks in the right place—a workplace that offers a sense of belonging and opportunity for the individual and profits for the organization.

Part I of *There Is No Place Like Work* presents the basics of CORE Culture in a modern business parable. You'll recognize its roots in *The Wonderful Wizard of Oz*. This story is a suitable metaphor for understanding culture and the importance of creating a workplace where employees feel at home at work. Part II begins with a brief description of the research that is the basis for our work and then covers critical steps in CORE Culture Management. Drawing from our clients' experiences, we've created cases and examples to show you how to harness the Five Ps, a set of key parameters delineating critical elements of your organization: Purpose, Philosophy, Priorities, Practices and Projections. We walk you through developing your company's CORE Culture Map, which gives you a visual emblem of your organization's identity and core principles. Then, we brief you on how to align your organization to the CORE Culture.

Our intent as authors is straightforward: to help you understand and shape your organization's CORE Culture step-by-step. Having leaders with a mastery of CORE Culture Management fulfills every organization's goal: to prosper as it seeks to continuously accomplish its authentic Purpose. Now, step onto our metaphorical Yellow Brick Road, and join us on the journey to a workplace you and your employees can call home.

PROLOGUE

WE all know the story of Dorothy and *The Wonderful Wizard of Oz*. This enduring tale depicts Dorothy's many adventures as she searches for her way back home.

But what if the story were different? What if Dorothy were searching for a way to create a workplace she and her employees could call home? What if she could discover the Wizard's lessons in a new way?

PART I

A Workplace to Call Home

CHAPTER 1

In Search of a
Better Workplace

FROM the moment Dot walked through the large double doors, she knew that something was amiss. As founder and CEO of Three Click Express, a travel company, Dot was accustomed to good and bad days. Recently, however, every day seemed to be a struggle. Nothing was easy or fun anymore. Dot placed her briefcase on the desk and sat down dejectedly.

"Good morning," Glinda, Dot's dedicated office manager, greeted her. "Just want to remind you of your new client meeting this morning with Mr. Steel at Heartland Pharmaceuticals. The company is looking for an incentive travel program to reward employees. Also," she added, "here are our latest sales figures for your review."

Dot took the papers from Glinda and quickly skimmed them—bad news again. This year's numbers were down and projections for next quarter were not looking any better. Expenses were continuing to rise and employee morale was at an all-time low. Dot wondered how her adventure travel company had come to this.

She looked out her office window and thought back to

the early years of Three Click Express. Dot recalled the days when she was involved in every facet of the business and knew each employee by name. People were enthusiastic and committed to their work. They formed a family of workers who cared about their customers and about each other. They had a passion for their cause and a sense of community. That had been a very satisfying time in her life.

Nowadays, the building seemed filled with strangers who were never content. Problems and complaints consumed every day. With profits down, Dot felt like the captain of a sinking ship. Somewhere along the way, Three Click had lost something, and she was determined to get it back.

Dot stirred from her thoughts as Glinda entered her office again. "Pardon me," she said. "Mr. Mayor is here, but he doesn't have an appointment."

"No problem," Dot said. "Please send him in!"

Mr. Mayor, Dot's lifelong mentor, had always given her excellent advice.

"I hope I'm not disturbing you," Mr. Mayor said as he entered.

"Oh no. Actually your timing is perfect," she assured him.

Mr. Mayor noticed Dot's troubled expression and asked, "Things not going so well at Three Click Express?"

"That's an understatement. Our profits are falling and we've made cuts everywhere we can. Nothing seems to be able to stop this downward spiral."

Mr. Mayor looked at Dot solemnly. He knew that she had started Three Click Express with little more than a dream and had built a remarkable organization. She was a skillful leader: smart, visionary and responsive to the needs of employees and customers alike. Now the momentum had shifted, and he understood her concern.

"I know someone who might be able to help," Mr. Mayor suggested. "His name is Mr. Insite, and he lives near Reflection City. He has successfully advised other companies with similar issues. He's practically a wizard!"

"If Mr. Insite knows how to get Three Click back on track, I'd sure like to meet him," Dot said.

"Well, he's somewhat of a recluse. He primarily conducts research, but sometimes he'll meet with visitors at his private lodge," Mr. Mayor explained. "He doesn't accept phone calls. My understanding is that you just have to go there, and if it's a good time for him, he will meet with you."

"That's odd," Dot remarked.

"It is," Mr. Mayor agreed with a chuckle, "but that may be his intention. Sometimes we learn the most about ourselves when we try something that's not so comfortable, when we take a strange or different path, even one that may appear to be a mistake. Times like this often hold great potential for learning and discovering those things that are most meaningful."

Dot sat pensively for a moment. Three Click Express was at a critical point, and nothing she had tried so far had made a difference. Maybe Mr. Insite would have some answers.

"Sounds like a great idea. I'll go to Reflection City today," Dot said with resolve.

"Good luck on your quest," Mr. Mayor said, rising from the chair. "Oh, I almost forgot." He handed Dot a small package. "I saw this and thought you might like it."

She opened the unexpected gift to find a small journal: a book of blank pages uniquely bound in a shiny silver cover. "How thoughtful," she said, thumbing through the pages. "Thank you. Now, if only this book had the answers I need."

"I'm sure you'll find your answers," Mr. Mayor said confidently, leaving Dot's office as unobtrusively as he had come.

Dot placed the journal in her briefcase and immediately began to prepare for her trip. "Glinda, I need directions to the office of a Mr. Insite near Reflection City," she said.

Within seconds her trusted office manager reappeared. "Just follow the Golden Highway due south," Glinda said, putting a piece of paper with detailed instructions on Dot's desk.

"If I'm not mistaken," Dot recalled, "Mane Industries is also on the Golden Highway near Reflection City."

Glinda nodded knowingly. "They're one of our best customers, and we almost lost that account last month to our strongest competitor."

"Exactly. Why don't you arrange a meeting for me on my way?" Dot tucked the directions into her new journal and walked to the door. "First, I'll go to my appointment at Heartland Pharmaceuticals. If I don't hear from you to the contrary, I'll stop by Mane Industries on my way to Reflection City. Call me if you need me."

AND THE JOURNEY BEGINS . . .

CHAPTER 2

In Search of Meaning
–The Purpose

THE opportunity to meet with Heartland Pharmaceuticals couldn't have come at a better time, Dot thought, as she turned onto the Golden Highway. *This new account could be just what we need.*

When she saw the Heartland Pharmaceuticals building looming imposingly before her, Dot exited the highway. She entered the underground garage at the base of the soaring glass structure, parked and took the elevator to the lobby. As Dot approached the reception desk, she found herself immersed in a swell of energy and motion. Set against a background of sleek granite and glass, clusters of people in white lab coats scurried by, engaged in lively discussion. A swarm of visitors gathered at the reception desk. Dot took a place at the end of the line and tried to absorb the animated scene. Even the large mobiles that hung from the towering ceiling were in constant motion. Finally, she made her way to the receptionist.

"Hello. I'm here to see Mr. Steel," Dot said to the gentleman sitting behind the large desk. "I'm from Three Click Express."

Mr. Steel has been expecting you. You'll find him in his office down the corridor to your right," the receptionist directed.

Dot followed the hall to an airy, sun-drenched room with windows that looked down to the busy city street. "Hi. I'm Dot from Three Click Express," she said.

A tall, thin man with metallic gray eyes and silver hair rose gracefully from his chair to greet her. "I'm Mr. Steel," he said cordially as he shook her hand and offered her a seat.

"Thank you for seeing me," Dot said, taking a chair facing his desk.

"It's my pleasure," Mr. Steel replied. "I've been looking forward to meeting you."

"I wanted the opportunity to come by in person so I could better understand Heartland Pharmaceuticals and the services you're looking for," she explained, opening her briefcase. "At Three Click, we create custom discovery travel experiences for each of our clients. By learning about your company and the people who work here, we can design incentive travel adventures that are tailored to your needs. These materials describe some of our capabilities," Dot said, handing him a large packet.

"What an impressive service," he said as he reviewed the information.

"It's just the way we do things at Three Click Express," Dot informed him proudly. Then she added, "So tell me about your work at Heartland Pharmaceuticals. From my brief time in the lobby, I can see that this is a very dynamic company."

"Oh, it is. I love working here," he said.

"Really? What makes Heartland so special?"

"Our work is extremely challenging and meaningful," Mr. Steel said zealously. "We have an exceptional company filled with people who are dedicated to improving health and the quality of life. We seek to cure diseases, ease suffering and promote longer, healthier and happier lives. We do more good for more people than any other pharmaceutical company in the world. That's why I came to Heartland, and that's why I stay."

"How inspiring. Have you been with Heartland for a long time?" Dot asked.

"I've been here about three years. I worked for another company for quite a while, but I was never really satisfied. Something was missing. I did my job well and I was successful, but my heart wasn't in it. Then one day, as luck would have it, my company downsized and I lost my job."

"How was that lucky?"

"Often, things that seem to be misfortunes at first turn out to hold unexpected possibilities. When I lost my job, I didn't know what direction to take. Then I realized that I had the opportunity to make a critical decision. It all became clear once I thought about the Purpose of work from the inside out."

"What do you mean?"

Pausing for a moment, Mr. Steel said, "I'd like to draw a picture for you that might make it easier to understand."

"Good idea." Dot reached into her briefcase and handed him the journal Mr. Mayor had given her, the sunlight dancing off its shiny silver cover. "Please use this," she offered.

"All right," he said, opening the book. "Now let me explain. It all begins with understanding the Purpose."

"Purpose?" Dot repeated curiously.

The man sketched a circle and wrote . . .

"People seek meaning in their lives; and they want the opportunity to make a difference. Because you spend so much of your life at work, your job should be a source of inspiration and an avenue for self-actualization. It should satisfy your need to make the world a better place. If your work is to be truly meaningful, understanding your organization's Purpose is central."

Dot nodded, "Please go on."

"I realized that I needed to find a place where my work would feel meaningful. I have always been interested in health and medicine. Not just in maintaining health, but in finding real solutions to improving the quality of life. That's why I came to Heartland Pharmaceuticals. Here I can do that—*preserve and enhance life*. I do a job I love for a company that saves lives and improves the health of millions of people around the world. I take personal pride in the impact our pharmaceuticals have on the lives of others. I know that each day our work makes someone's life better. This is more than just a business; it's a cause that really matters to me."

"I can see that you love your work," Dot commented.

"When you search for a place to do your work, pick one that feels right for you—a company whose Purpose fits your passion." He pointed to his drawing. "You see, organizations are centered around a Purpose. The Purpose serves as a magnet, drawing people together to make their impact on the world. It's like a guiding star whose light attracts, inspires commitment and provides a shared focus."

Mr. Steel wrote . . .

Purpose

**The Purpose
of an organization
is the fundamental
reason it exists**

"We know why organizations exist," Dot chuckled, reading the words in the circle. "All companies exist to make money. That's pretty obvious."

Mr. Steel smiled and said, "Of course, most organizations exist to make money. Otherwise, they could not stay in business. But making money is not what we mean by Purpose. The Purpose is more than just making money; it's the heart of the organization. Making money is important, but it's not usually what makes people feel fulfilled. Here at Heartland Pharmaceuticals, our Purpose is improving the lives of people. The Purpose of an organization is the cause for which it was created, the cause that gives members a chance to make a difference through their work."

Dot looked squarely at Mr. Steel. "So, if you know the Purpose of a company and if that Purpose is a cause that you connect to personally, then maybe you've found the workplace that's right for you?"

"Exactly," he confirmed. "In successful organizations, the Purpose of the organization is also the Purpose of its members. When the Purpose is genuinely owned and shared by members, the feeling of unity and collective spirit propels the organization toward success."

"That makes sense," Dot agreed. "If you think about the things that are important to you, then you can determine if an organization is a good fit. If you don't feel personally connected to its Purpose, then maybe you need to work someplace else."

"Correct," Mr. Steel said. "When members feel connected to the Purpose, the combined energy is quite remarkable. But when that connection is missing or when you don't have the same passion as your colleagues, it just won't feel right. When you're searching for the place to do your work, seek a place that allows you to express yourself in a way that matters to you. That is the initial step in finding a workplace that brings you happiness and success, and contributes to leading a meaningful life."

"It certainly appears you've found that here," Dot said.

"I have," Mr. Steel responded. "Heartland's Purpose is apparent not only in the work we do for others, but also in our workplace practices. It is important that we promote a work environment that fosters health and well-being. Therefore, on site we offer numerous benefits that improve the lives of our employees and their families. We have wellness programs, a recreation and fitness facility, a free health center and an elder-care referral program, just to name a few. Heartland is true to our Purpose of preserving and enhancing the lives of our employees as well as our customers."

"What a rewarding place to work," Dot acknowledged.

"It is wonderful. I have found a company that does the kind of work that personally matters to me. I am energized by my job, and I feel like I make a genuine contribution. Each day gives me an opportunity to preserve and enhance life. I'm not saying that this is the only place that would be right for me, but it sure is a great fit."

Dot sat quietly for a moment thinking about Three Click Express and the challenge before her. Then she asked, "So, how does a company discover its Purpose?"

"It's not a very complicated process," Mr. Steel assured Dot. "First ask yourself, 'What is the Purpose of this organization?' Then dig deeper by asking another question, 'Why is that important?' Sometimes you need to ask the second question several times to uncover your company's real Purpose. With each question, you get closer and closer to the essence of the organization."

"So once you know the Purpose, how exactly does that help you?" Dot asked.

"Once you understand the Purpose of the organization, it serves as a focus. It centers your thoughts and becomes the foundation for your actions," Mr. Steel explained.

"When the Purpose of the organization is clear, you must ask whether or not that Purpose is a cause that is meaningful to you. Here at Heartland Pharmaceuticals, we are dedicated to our Purpose—preserving and enhancing life—and that's a perfect match for me."

Mr. Steel wrote in Dot's journal . . .

HEARTLAND PHARMACEUTICALS

Purpose

To preserve and enhance life

Dot studied the words—to preserve and enhance life. "What a meaningful Purpose. Life-enhancing work is quite a cause. I can see why you're so passionate about this organization."

"I am," he replied warmly.

"Meeting you and learning about your organization has been invaluable," Dot said, returning the journal to her briefcase. "Now that I understand Heartland's Purpose, my team can create programs that will reinforce your organization's life-enhancing focus. I'll have some options designed for you to review. Can we speak again next week?"

"Sure. This has been a pleasure," Mr. Steel said as he helped Dot maneuver through the bustling lobby toward the front doors. "We have an extraordinary culture," he observed. "Each of us comes to work driven by our quest to help others. Even I am constantly amazed at how much energy is generated here."

"The activity is remarkable," Dot agreed as she shook Mr. Steel's hand. "Thank you for sharing the heart of your company with me."

AND THE JOURNEY CONTINUES . . .

CHAPTER 3

In Search of Distinctiveness —The Philosophy

BACK in her car once again and traveling down the Golden Highway, Dot watched Heartland Pharmaceuticals grow smaller and smaller in her rearview mirror. As she drove, she reviewed her conversation with Mr. Steel about an organization's Purpose. Maybe the lack of a clear Purpose, she thought, is something we need to address at Three Click. She pondered how much better things would be if all employees could be as enthusiastic about their work as Mr. Steel.

Looking up the road ahead, Dot noticed something very strange. Driving closer, she saw a group of buildings shaped like oversized children's blocks. The buildings were painted a variety of primary colors and randomly connected by semitransparent, yellow tubular walkways. Manicured lawns curved among the buildings. Shaded benches, picnic tables and duck ponds were scattered amid the landscape.

"I wonder what they do here," Dot said aloud as she came to a complete stop in front of the unusual complex. Then she noticed a small sign: VISITORS WELCOME. Without hesitation, Dot parked her car and walked toward the entrance. Large glass doors opened into the center of a dome-shaped lobby. Above her the sunlight filtered through multicolored skylights, drenching the white stone floor in a kaleidoscope of rainbows and prisms.

"May I help you?" asked an inquisitive voice coming from the speaker above.

Dot turned around but saw no one. "I'm a visitor. I was interested in the building and what you do here," Dot said awkwardly as she spoke into thin air.

"Someone will be with you in a moment," the voice responded cheerfully.

Almost immediately, a gangly young man emerged from a side corridor and sprinted toward her. He had wild, straw-colored hair that stood up from his head in every direction. His cheeks were flushed pink, and his eyes were the color of the sky.

"Hi," he smiled broadly. "My name is Ignatius Quinn, but everyone calls me I.Q. I hear you'd like to see our company."

"I would," Dot said. "Please tell me, what do you do here?"

"We design toys!" he replied enthusiastically.

"A toy company?" Dot questioned.

"Well, in a way, but not a typical toy company," he explained. "If you'll follow me, I'll show you how we work at Intellitoy." The young man bounded toward a corridor, and Dot found herself rushing to keep up with him. I.Q. led Dot down a bright yellow passage to an elevator that climbed to the second floor and opened onto a suspended walkway. "You'll be able to see things much better from up here," he said with a grin.

Dot ventured out onto the platform. An elaborate web of catwalks seemed to extend endlessly above the ground level. She gazed below in amazement as myriads of people scurried among opalescent domes that lay like giant sea shells on the polished concrete floor. Small groups of observers watched as children played happily with cyber robots, virtual synthesizers and holographic games. Dot heard laughter ripple through the air as clusters of people, talking and gesturing with enthusiasm, hovered over massive tables. The casual dress and lighthearted manner of every-one gave Dot the feeling that she was looking at a play-ground rather than a work environment.

"I've never seen anything like this before," Dot said.

"And you probably never will," the wild-haired man said proudly. "At Intellitoy, we make fun smart. We believe that people of all ages have the capacity to enjoy and to learn. Everything you see here is designed to help us remember that."

"What are they doing?" Dot asked, pointing to the seemingly chaotic scene below.

"They're developing new ideas. This is where it all starts—in what we call the Brain Pit."

"Interesting name," Dot said.

"It's an even more interesting process. Here, our thinkers' minds can run free; nothing is out of bounds, and everything is within the realm of possibility. The only rule we have is to invent ways to have fun while expanding intelligence."

"Did I understand you correctly? Did you call the employees 'thinkers'?" Dot asked.

"Certainly! That's who we are," he responded, leading her further along the walkway. "We are hired to use our minds, our imaginations. And each of us takes that responsibility quite seriously."

"Seriously?" Dot asked. "Everyone looks like they're having such a good time; it's hard to believe that any work is actually getting done."

"That's the idea," I.Q. laughed. "Our work is our fun, and we're in the business of promoting fun." He led her to a very large landing encased in opaque panels. "After you," he said, opening the door. "This is our Relaxation Station."

Stepping inside the enclosure, Dot tried to take in the scene before her. A series of flat screen monitors covered a large wall. Headphones and keyboards sat in recessed racks below the screens. Comfortable, brightly colored chairs were scattered throughout the room along with tables of varying shapes and sizes. Each tile in the metallic floor was imprinted with the Intellitoy logo. Dot suddenly became aware that the air was filled with the aroma of freshly brewed coffee, emanating from the refreshment stand in the center of the room.

"Help yourself," I.Q. said, pointing to the refreshment center.

"That would be great," Dot said, making her selection. "So tell me, have you worked here long?"

"Only a few years, but what an incredible few years it's been. I'm working for the most amazing person. She's brilliant, a true visionary, and without a doubt, the reason I'm here," I.Q. admitted.

"Really?" Dot asked with heightened interest.

"If you heard her talk for just a few moments, you'd understand what I mean. She speaks so quickly, shifting from thought to thought, always generating new ideas. I have never met anyone as smart. Her unique intellect impresses me all the time. That's why coming to work here was really a no-brainer."

Dot was as intrigued with I.Q.'s exhilarating manner as she was with his story. "So you decided to work here when you met her?" Dot asked.

"Yes, but let me explain. I've always had a fascination with toys. I guess I'm like a kid who never grew up. I looked around and interviewed with a number of companies. While they were all involved in some way with designing toys, something didn't fit for me. Then I interviewed with the CEO here and realized the difference: this company uses brainpower to promote fun. That's what I was looking for, although I didn't realize it until I came here. All employees at Intellitoy are encouraged to experiment and play while they create the most intelligent toys. Once I understood this, I knew Intellitoy was the place for me."

Dot thought back to her conversation with Mr. Steel at Heartland Pharmaceuticals. "So what you're saying is that the Purpose of Intellitoy is to promote fun?" She took her journal from her briefcase and showed I.Q. the picture of the circle with the word Purpose.

"You got it—our Purpose is *to promote fun*. But the Purpose alone does not reflect the total picture of our company. To understand better, you need to draw another circle. Do you mind if I show you?" he asked Dot.

"That would be great," she replied.

"Please have a seat," he said.

Dot sat down and handed him the journal.

I.Q. began to explain, "If you know the Purpose of an organization, that's the beginning. But there's another component that's just as critical—the Philosophy."

He drew a larger circle around the Purpose and wrote the word Philosophy inside it.

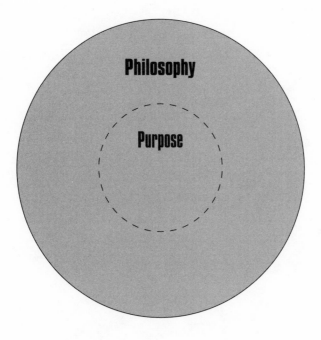

"With a Purpose there must also be a Philosophy. An organization possesses its own distinctive character that defines it and sets it apart from others. And that unique character is the Philosophy."

I.Q. wrote . . .

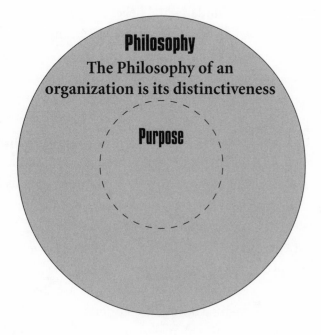

"The Philosophy is an organization's distinctiveness and the basis for its individuality," he said. "It is the reason two companies in the same business can be so different. The Philosophy gives an organization's Purpose its spirit and affects how you do your work. Here at Intellitoy, our Philosophy is the fundamental belief in the importance of *intelligence*. Intelligence is central to everything we do."

"What a smart business to be in. Intelligence-promoting toys are always in demand," Dot said.

"They are," I.Q. replied. "And we design an extensive line of educational toys based on the latest research. We create toys that make complex topics—from physics, to finance, to neurology—not only fun but also informative. We partner with high-tech companies to infuse their inventive ideas into our toys. Our expanded line of toys engages, enlightens and educates even our youngest customers."

"Intelligent toys for babies?" Dot asked.

"Yes, we are proud of our new Intellibooks that teach foreign languages to little ones before they are able to read. And they love them. All Intellitoys offer a variety of entertaining and educational experiences. Everything we do makes fun smart."

I.Q. wrote in Dot's journal . . .

INTELLITOY

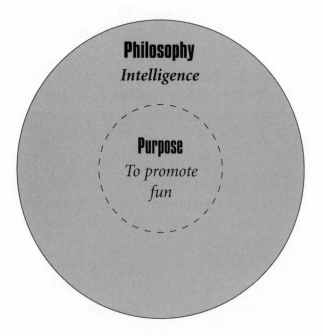

Philosophy
Intelligence

Purpose
To promote fun

"Interesting," Dot said, intrigued by her guide's perspective. "How does an organization develop its Philosophy?"

"Generally, the Philosophy stems from the founder or leader. That's certainly the case at Intellitoy where our CEO has created a company that mirrors her intelligence and constant yearning to learn. This intellectual focus is obvious in every action she takes, and it filters down to everyone who works here. The Intellitoy Philosophy is very real to her, and it's something we all connect with, believe in and work to support. Unless people share this intellectual focus, they probably won't enjoy working here."

Dot thought about the enthusiasm that had energized her company in the beginning and the many employees who were now dissatisfied. "So when you are looking for work, it's important to find a place with a Purpose and Philosophy that fit who you are," Dot said.

"That's the way I see it," he agreed, his sky blue eyes sparkling. "No company is going to be a perfect fit. But the key is to find one that supports who you are and what you think is important."

"Makes sense," Dot nodded thoughtfully.

"The Purpose and the Philosophy are the foundation and the framework of the organization," I.Q. continued. "The Purpose alone may not be distinctive. Many organizations may share a similar Purpose. But when the Purpose is delivered in a distinctive way—guided by the Philosophy—that's a special combination."

"I can see that understanding the Purpose and the

Philosophy of a company is crucial to building a successful organization," Dot agreed.

"Absolutely," I.Q. said encouragingly.

"This is an exceptional place, and I've learned a lot," Dot said. "Clearly, this very smart and fun company is very successful." Then, glancing at her watch, she added, "I've taken up so much of your time. Thank you, I.Q., for the tour and the insights."

I.Q. handed the journal back to Dot. "It's been a pleasure meeting you," he said cheerfully as he walked Dot through the lobby and back to the entrance. "Every time I have the opportunity to show someone Intellitoy, it reminds me how much I enjoy working here. I hope you've had fun, too!"

AND THE JOURNEY CONTINUES . . .

CHAPTER 4

In Search of Values —The Priorities

AS Dot drove down the Golden Highway, she considered the unique environment she had experienced at Intellitoy. Understanding an organization's Purpose and Philosophy, she thought, is important for both the organization and its employees. They define the essence of the organization and its distinction.

Rounding a sharp curve a few miles later, Dot saw the buildings of Mane Industries sprawled out before her. "Mane certainly has grown!" she exclaimed aloud. Dot pulled her car into a grand gated entrance marked by a large sign: MANE INDUSTRIES—CORPORATE HEADQUARTERS. A uniformed guard promptly approached her car, checked his list and pointed her toward the visitors' parking area.

Walking from her car, Dot was astonished as she surveyed her surroundings. Mane Industries appeared to be set in a jungle. The vegetation was dense and exotic. Waterfalls, streams and ponds dotted the landscape, flowers bloomed from every bed and colorful birds flew overhead, perching now and then on lush verdant trees. Beautifully pebbled pathways, covered by emerald green canopies, connected the large stone buildings.

Dot followed a series of small wood-carved signs to the main building. Enormous stone lions sat on both sides of the majestic wooden doors, which were inscribed, THE COURAGE TO BE THE BEST. Dot entered an immense terrarium-like lobby filled with the most striking plant life she had ever seen.

"Hello," Dot said, approaching the security desk. "I'm here to see Mr. Mane. I'm from Three Click Express."

"I'll tell him you're here," the uniformed man replied. Within moments the man directed Dot to the glass elevator toward the rear of the lobby.

The elevator climbed to the top floor where Dot followed a wide, windowed corridor to another set of large wooden doors. Mr. Mane, a big, burly man with a blond beard and mustache, greeted her immediately. Despite his massive stature, he strode across the floor almost soundlessly. "Dot!" he roared. "What a great pleasure to see you!"

"It's good to see you, too," she replied warmly.

"What brings you to our neck of the woods?" he asked, offering her a chair.

"I know we spoke at length last month to resolve the issues you had with Three Click, but I wanted to meet face-to-face to ensure your total satisfaction. We consider ourselves your partner in business, and we take pride in providing personal service. At Three Click we have a genuine interest in the well-being of our customers."

Mr. Mane paced back and forth in front of the large windows that encircled his office. "I appreciate your personal interest. Everything is running smoothly now," he declared. "I trust you will continue doing all you can to provide excellent service. We have built a company at Mane Industries that accepts nothing less than the best from our people, from our partners, from our vendors and for our customers. Excellence is our primary focus, but it is not always easy for others to understand or accept that. We see it as an inspiring challenge."

"Well, it certainly has worked for you," Dot remarked approvingly. "Your business seems to be flourishing."

"It has, indeed, been a satisfying experience," the imposing man said graciously. "We started with a passion to be the best, and we moved into the industry with a determination to compete at a level that had never before been attempted."

"I heard that Mane Industries set a new standard of excellence in this industry," Dot said respectfully. "How did you do it?"

"The key to our success is our competitiveness," explained Mr. Mane in a commanding voice. "You might say we have a relentless appetite for competition. We constantly seek better ways to enhance our products, so we can help our customers compete and be highly successful. You see, we're driven; we never stop pursuing excellence. We see ourselves as the most ferocious competitor in our industry. We only perform at peak levels where our competition becomes our prey. If you look around, our campus is filled with a diverse collection of aggressive, innovative risk takers.

We could not have achieved this level of success without those values."

"This sounds similar to some things I've heard recently about Purpose and Philosophy," Dot said, reaching into her briefcase and opening her journal.

"Mmmm, very interesting," Mr. Mane said, as he took the journal and reviewed the drawings and comments. "At Mane Industries, our Purpose is *to promote excellence.* As the leading manufacturer of athletic gear, we are in the business of helping others be the best. And that Purpose is directed by our Philosophy, our fundamental belief in the importance of *competition.* Competitiveness is our distinctive trait in this industry, and for me, it is also instinctive. I've always thrived on a competitive spirit."

"Striving for excellence through competition," Dot repeated, encouraging him to say more.

"Correct!" Mr. Mane bellowed. "Our passion for excellence and our competitive nature describe life at Mane Industries. That is the essence of who we are. But, additionally, a few key values further guide our work. Those are our Priorities. Let me show you."

He drew another circle and wrote the word Priorities.

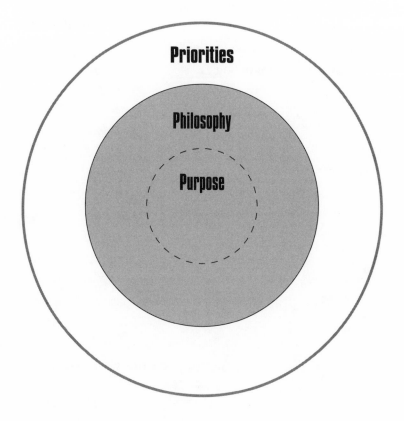

"Surrounding the Purpose and the Philosophy are the organization's Priorities," he explained. "The Priorities are core values that set the standards for behavior. They guide how everyone puts the Purpose and the Philosophy into practice in day-to-day activities."

He wrote the following . . .

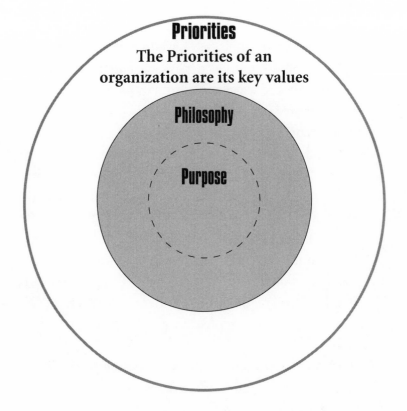

"We believe that we can best achieve our passion for excellence with a competitive spirit by adhering to a specific set of Priorities," he said.

"So what are Mane Industries' Priorities?" Dot asked.

"We believe our employees have to be *aggressive,* constantly demonstrating drive, persistence and perseverance, so we can promote excellence through competition. Our people never give up; they always give their best.

"The second Priority that we live by is *risk taking.* Employees don't have to get permission for every decision they make. We pursue success without fear of failure. If you don't have the courage to take risks, you can't be the king of the forest. So we don't just allow risk taking, we highly encourage it.

"We conquer our competition by providing superior products, so *innovation* is also a vital Priority. We set the standard for creating product ideas that others never even imagine, and we aggressively get those new products to market.

"And, of course, our Priority of *customer service* is essential in business today. If we don't get repeat business from our customers, we've failed."

Mr. Mane sketched in the journal . . .

MANE INDUSTRIES

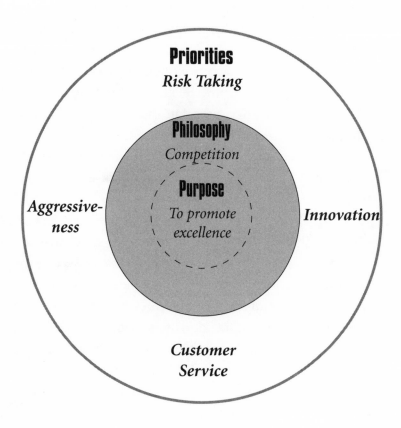

"I can see that these values work well for Mane Industries," Dot said.

Mr. Mane nodded his shaggy head with confidence. "They do. Our Priorities—aggressiveness, risk taking, innovation and customer service—are the key values that guide our work. When we constantly apply these standards, they enable us to achieve and promote excellence. At Mane Industries, we've accomplished remarkable success by following these Priorities. Being the competitive creatures that we are, we like that a lot."

"How do you ensure everyone shares these values?"

"Each person we hire understands the company's values," he confirmed. "That's how we've created a pack-like culture."

"How does that work?" Dot asked.

"Well, when we hire, we look for more than just a person's ability to do a particular job. We select people who are already customer-focused, aggressive, risk-taking innovators. We seek distinctively competitive employees who naturally demonstrate those values and who have the desire and passion to be the best. After the selection process, our individual orientation and training aggressively reinforce these traits. Our employees have diverse styles and talents. However, they each have a personal commitment to our Priorities, and they know that these Priorities are the critical standards that govern their work. We believe that if we select the right people, they will behave this way effortlessly. It is as instinctive for them as it is for me."

"I don't think most companies are as aggressive in their selection and training as you are," Dot said.

"You're probably right," Mr. Mane agreed.

"Actually," Dot said, "everyone should be selective."

"This is true. Job seekers and those who have jobs should be selective, too," he confirmed. "It is essential to determine if one's values are compatible with the Priorities of the organization. Priorities set the standards of behavior, and if one finds those values incompatible, it is wise to ask if that workplace is really the right place. Differing values can cause fierce problems. Here at Mane Industries, applicants who don't identify with our Priorities either do not get hired, or quickly self-select out of our company."

"So do Priorities ever change?" questioned Dot.

"Priorities can change to be competitive," Mr. Mane answered. "For instance, in the past we valued control through a strict chain of command. But today business moves much too fast. So we consciously shifted to embrace risk taking, which more effectively positions us to be the best."

"So, that change in Priorities was driven by your company's competitive nature," Dot responded.

"In successful organizations," he continued, "the wisdom lies in changing the Priorities when necessary, but not in changing the Purpose or the Philosophy—that is, unless you're seeking revolutionary change. Changes in the Priorities have an impact on the organization, but they don't produce radical change as long as the new values are consistent with the Purpose and the Philosophy."

"So a company's Priorities can be somewhat flexible, if necessary," Dot summarized, "while the Purpose and the Philosophy remain stable."

"You got it," Mr. Mane replied.

"I understand how your Priorities have helped you compete," Dot added.

"When everyone's actions support the Priorities," Mr. Mane explained, "the result can be quite powerful."

"Mr. Mane, this discussion has been very informative," Dot said appreciatively. "Thank you so much."

Mr. Mane closed Dot's journal and handed it to her. "Thank you for taking the time to personally check on things. I can tell that Three Click also values customer service."

"We do. And I'm sure Three Click Express will be able to provide the exceptional service you expect," she said as Mr. Mane walked with her to the elevator. "It has been a pleasure seeing you again." Dot shook his hand. "If you're ever out our way, I do hope you'll stop by."

"An excellent idea," Mr. Mane roared as the elevator doors closed.

AND THE JOURNEY CONTINUES . . .

CHAPTER **5**

In Search of Insight
—Understanding the CORE

DRIVING through the grand gates of Mane Industries, Dot resumed her journey down the Golden Highway. Soon she detected something sparkling beyond the horizon. That must be Reflection City, she assumed, driving a little faster. Within moments it came into view—buildings, bridges and highways seemingly laced together to create a silver lattice-like pattern across the entire glistening city. As she drew closer, Dot observed that most of the surfaces were covered in mirrors or shiny metals that shimmered in the sunlight. Everything appeared to sparkle with a magical luminescence. The radiant city seemed to grow magnificently before her eyes as she got closer.

The Golden Highway carried Dot toward the center of Reflection City. Reviewing her directions once more, she veered onto a narrow road, spiraling toward the top of a mountain. The road turned from pavement to gravel and then abruptly ended, depositing her onto a dirt clearing near the mountain peak. Dot stopped the car, took out her directions and examined them again. "I followed these directions exactly," she said aloud, "so Mr. Insite's lodge should be close by."

Deciding to look around, Dot walked to the edge of the mountaintop plateau and gazed at the sparkling city far below. Though the air was warm, a cool breeze rustled through the trees, and the sky shimmered with the last filtered rays of the late afternoon sun.

Dot began to reflect on her journey. She retraced the encounters she had experienced along the way and the lessons she had learned about Purpose at Heartland Pharmaceuticals, Philosophy at Intellitoy and Priorities at Mane Industries.

She recalled Mr. Mayor's words: *Sometimes we learn the most about ourselves when we try something that's not so comfortable, when we take a strange or different path, even one that may appear to be a mistake. Times like this often hold great potential for learning and discovering those things that are most meaningful.* Dot realized how valuable her travels had been so far.

Through a small bank of trees, Dot detected a hint of flickering light. Perhaps that's the place, she thought, taking her briefcase and heading toward the light. Soon she reached an open space in the woods where tall lanterns illuminated a sprawling timber-and-glass house nestled on a beautiful lake. Although the lodge was imposing, it seemed to blend gracefully with its setting.

Dot approached the lodge door, but before she could knock, it swung open. "Welcome," a man in a plaid shirt and jeans greeted her. "I saw you pull into our clearing a while ago. May I help you?"

"Yes, thank you. I'm looking for Mr. Insite's lodge," Dot explained.

"Well, you've found it," the man confirmed.

"Great. Do you know if Mr. Insite is available? I'd like to speak with him about my company."

"I am Mr. Insite," he responded.

"Oh, I'm very glad to meet you. My name is Dot," she said, shaking his hand.

"Come in, please," Mr. Insite offered. "You've actually come at an opportune time."

Dot entered and looked around the vast, richly paneled room. Scattered among numerous computer workstations were clusters of cozy couches and overstuffed chairs. Books filled every available space from the tops of tables to the large shelves that covered the walls. The sound of classical music drifted gently through the air. Dot felt as if she had been transported to another dimension.

"This is an unusual place," Dot said. "Is this where you do your work?"

"Yes, it is. I constructed this lodge to facilitate insightful thinking, to be totally aligned with my Purpose, which is to promote a more insightful world. I work with a cadre of associates. Frequently, I meet with business and government leaders to guide them in promoting insightfulness in their work. What I do here is very stimulating. It's more than a business; it's my life's work."

Mr. Insite led Dot past a massive staircase to the back porch where they stood with a full view of the evening sky and a lake that stretched out before them. Offering her one of the rocking chairs, he said, "Now, Dot, I know you want to talk to me about something specific. What seems to be the issue?"

Dot felt a sense of relief as she began to describe her concerns. "My adventure travel company, Three Click Express, was once a thriving, successful and stimulating place to work. Yet, over the past few years, it has become something very different. Somehow I have not managed to preserve what made it so special. Our profits are down, our customers are dissatisfied and our employees are not performing. We've lost the enthusiasm that made us great, and I don't know how to turn things around."

"I have found that people frequently know much more about their situations than they initially think. Give yourself a moment to reflect. I'm sure you have some ideas about how to make things better," Mr. Insite said encouragingly.

"Well, perhaps," Dot responded as she took out her journal.

"What an unusual book," Mr. Insite observed.

"Thank you. It was a gift from a friend," she explained.

"Gifts are quite special," he said. "They are wonderful opportunities to show appreciation. And, just as people give gifts to each other, companies like Three Click Express also give gifts to the world."

"I think I have an idea of what you mean," Dot said, opening the book.

"Then, tell me," Mr. Insite requested, "what is the gift that your company offers? What does your company do to make this world better? That gift is its Purpose, the source of meaning not only for Three Click but also for each person who works there. Without a clear understanding of that Purpose, it is quite difficult to preserve the passion that your company once had."

"You know, I met someone on my way here who described Purpose to me," Dot said as she turned to the drawings in the journal. "He said that the Purpose of an organization is the fundamental reason it exists. Purpose is the cause that people feel passionately connected to."

"Precisely. So why does your company exist? What is the Purpose of Three Click Express?" questioned Mr. Insite.

"I guess you might say we provide travel services," Dot answered. "That's our Purpose."

"Okay, you provide travel services," reflected Mr. Insite. "Why is that important?"

"I believe it's important for people to have the opportunity to see the world," responded Dot.

"And why is that important?" questioned Mr. Insite once again.

Dot sat for a moment deep in thought. "I believe that through travel, people can experience adventure. Travel to new and different places takes people out of their normal surroundings."

"And why is that important?" he asked another time.

"It's important because adventure travel pushes people in a way that encourages them to grow and expand their perspectives. At Three Click Express, we help our customers experience the thrill of an adventure and encounter the wonder of new places—it's a discovery and self-discovery process at the same time." Dot paused for a moment. "Yes, that's right. Our Purpose is *to provide the experience of discovery.*"

"That is a very meaningful Purpose," Mr. Insite acknowledged.

"It fits for me," Dot said. "In fact, it's been a central focus of my life for quite awhile."

"How's that?" he inquired.

"Well, I grew up on a farm on the outskirts of a small town where I lived with my aunt and uncle. As a child, I never had any particular interest in leaving home and exploring the world. But, as fate would have it, one day I was forced to embark on a journey to a faraway land. It was a profound and amazing adventure. When I returned home, I realized that this experience had not only given me a broader view of the world, but also a clearer sense of myself. It was a transforming event in my life. I think that's why providing the experience of discovery for our customers is so important to me, and why I started this company. I wanted to assist others in their journeys toward discovery of the world and them-selves." Then, feeling slightly self-conscious, Dot added,

"Why did it take me so long to describe Three Click's Purpose? You would think, after all this time, I would know it."

"That is the way it works. It always requires multiple questions to get to the real Purpose. Often people describe their organization's Purpose as something that is too limiting," Mr. Insite explained. "If we had stayed with your first response—to provide travel services—it would have been too narrow. You never know what things will be like even five years from now, much less fifty. Maybe in the future your Purpose—providing the experience of discovery— will entail something other than travel services."

"Absolutely," Dot agreed. "Things change so rapidly. I can see how a narrowly defined Purpose can limit your view of a company and its work."

"Precisely. You must keep your Purpose brief in length and broad in scope. This yields a Purpose that endures because it has elasticity and the capacity to adapt over time, while remaining constant and faithful to its central focus."

"I understand. When we first began our company, we said we were in the travel business. But we wanted to specialize in adventure travel. We targeted that type of business because of our desire to promote excitement, stimulation and a sense of adventure. Although we never talked about it, I can see now that the discovery process is the real reason we are in business. That focus is truly inspirational to us all. Unfortunately, even though it is so important, we have not taken the time to discuss it."

"Without consciously understanding your organization's gift to the world, you may not be as successful as you'd like," stressed Mr. Insite. "May I write something in your journal?"

"Of course," Dot said, handing him the shiny little book.

Mr. Insite turned to a blank page and wrote . . .

INSIGHT #1

The Purpose of an organization is the fundamental reason it exists.

• The Purpose is the cause that unites efforts and inspires action.

• The Purpose is brief in length and broad in scope.

• The Purpose is the answer to the question, "Why is this work important?"

"A Purpose is like a compass that provides direction for a journey that often has no end," Mr. Insite said, handing the journal back to Dot. "It is your chance to make a difference and be part of a meaningful legacy. Everyone in your organization must understand that Purpose and see it as their gift to the world through their work."

"At Three Click, providing the experience of discovery is our cause, the reason we are in business," Dot repeated thoughtfully.

"It is vital to constantly keep that Purpose alive in the hearts and minds of everyone who works at Three Click," cautioned Mr. Insite. "To be it, one must know it. The information that we allow into our consciousness determines the content and focus of our lives.

"But Purpose alone is not the total picture," he added. "Let me explain. Look at the cover of your journal."

Dot stared into the cover of the journal; the shiny exterior reflected a mirror image of her face.

Mr. Insite asked, "What do you see?"

Dot wondered, "What do you mean?"

"What do you see when you look at the cover of your journal?"

"Me, of course," she responded. "This journal is like a mirror, and what I see is my reflection. Why do you ask?"

"Because this is the second component in your search to make Three Click Express a more successful company," explained Mr. Insite. "What you see in the cover is your reflection. As the founder of Three Click, you have created a unique organization. Its uniqueness reflects who you are. When you understand your special attributes, you will discover the distinctiveness of Three Click Express: its Philosophy."

Dot thought again about Intellitoy, where she first learned about an organization's Philosophy. At Intellitoy everything exuded intelligence. It was definitely the driving force that energized their work. It was their spirit and the source of their distinctiveness. Everything they did was based on the desire to make fun smart.

Mr. Insite continued. "Tell me about yourself. How would you describe your personal Philosophy, the idea that serves as the framework for how your company operates?"

"I think the way I do things evolved from that incredible childhood journey. That was when I first recognized the importance of relationships, how trust and working together can get you through just about any situation. Even in my most recent travels, I encountered people who helped me discover more about myself. They taught me the importance of listening to my heart, expanding my brain and exhibiting courage. I genuinely believe that meaningful personal interaction enriches experience and enhances perspective. It's my concern for others—appreciating individuals for their special gifts and contributions—that serves as the framework for how I do my work."

"So how do these beliefs shape your work?" he asked.

"I believe that caring for an individual's personal needs is the beginning of the discovery process. If Three Click

Express doesn't understand our clients, we won't understand their perspectives with the clarity that we need to produce the most satisfying opportunity for discovery. Our work is based on the Philosophy that creating authentic experiences requires authentic relationships. Our clients are lifelong partners. We consider each assignment a unique and personal journey. Whether it is providing tailored learning experiences or accommodating varied physical abilities, our genuine concern about each individual's needs has always shaped the special way we do things."

"So," Mr. Insite explored, "Three Click Express helps people experience discovery through relationships. Is the importance of authentic relationships the fundamental belief that frames the way you conduct your business?"

"Yes, that is the essence of how we work."

"Does this focus make Three Click different from other companies with a similar Purpose?"

"Yes, I believe our attentiveness to people and the relationships that we develop with them make Three Click special," Dot confirmed. "Our Philosophy—our fundamental belief in the importance of *authentic relationships*—describes how we do business."

"As you see, the Philosophy can be a hard thing to label," Mr. Insite counseled. "The reason I asked about your personal Philosophy is because this organization is a reflection of you as the founder and leader."

"You've shown me that my genuine concern for authentic relationships directs how we do things at Three Click," Dot agreed, glancing again at the shiny cover of her journal.

"May I add to the journal once more?" Mr. Insite asked.

Dot handed the book to him, and he wrote . . .

INSIGHT #2

The Philosophy of an organization is its distinctiveness.

• The Philosophy is the prime belief that directs how business is conducted.

• The Philosophy is the organization's unique character that stems from the founder or leader.

• The Philosophy is the answer to the question, "What primary attribute makes this organization unique, special and different from other organizations with a similar Purpose?"

"The Philosophy is the central character of the organization and the organizing principle for how business is conducted," explained Mr. Insite. "It is the organization's distinctive feature and the prime attribute that members believe set it apart from the competition."

"I can see why understanding the Philosophy is so important for an organization," Dot commented.

"It is," Mr. Insite agreed. "The Philosophy intertwined with the Purpose is the basis for everything else. They are the anchors that ground an organization and the filters through which action is screened. Together they are the enduring traits that have defined the organization over the years."

"At Three Click," Dot suggested, "our Purpose is to promote the experience of discovery, driven by our Philosophy of authentic relationships."

"Exactly," replied Mr. Insite.

"Now I know what to preserve and promote," Dot said.

"You're right," Mr. Insite responded. "The Purpose defines 'why' the organization exists, and the Philosophy describes 'how' it delivers that Purpose. Just think of the Purpose and the Philosophy as your company's identity. Typically, loyal members of the company are connected to that identity. The Purpose alone is not usually distinctive, but the Purpose and Philosophy merge in a unique blend. When these two components are linked together as a unit, they define the organization's distinctive and enduring essence."

Mr. Insite then wrote . . .

INSIGHT #3

The combination of the Purpose and the Philosophy is the identity of an organization.

- Identity is the heart and soul of the organization.

- Identity is the anchor of the organization and the filter through which action is screened.

- The Purpose and the Philosophy together are the central and unique traits that have defined the organization over the years.

Dot added, "Our Purpose and Philosophy have always been fundamental to our organization."

"That's right," Mr. Insite said. "The Purpose confirms your valued cause, and the Philosophy identifies your unique character. They are central to your organization and everything must be consistent with them. These core elements are the heart and soul of your company. Pretty significant, don't you think?"

"Yes, indeed. And if these core elements are that important, then members of our company must view them similarly," Dot proposed.

"Precisely," agreed Mr. Insite. "And they must also feel a personal attachment to the Purpose and the Philosophy. Without that understanding and connection, you might not have the level of commitment and dedication Three Click needs to be an exceptional company."

"Now, I realize why we're having trouble. Everyone at Three Click must understand and be committed to our Purpose and Philosophy. It looks like I have a lot to do when I get back."

"Well, we're not quite finished," Mr. Insite said. "Although you've clearly defined the Purpose and the Philosophy of your company, there's more. A stable organizational identity serves as the core essence of the organization. But there must also be other elements that further guide the organization so that it can be effective in our world that so rapidly changes."

"This is beginning to sound complex," Dot said.

"It may sound complicated, but it's really quite simple. You've got it all right here," he reassured her, pointing to the journal.

Then Mr. Insite opened Dot's journal once again and a slip of paper fell to the ground. "Oh, sorry," Mr. Insite said as he reached down for it.

"No problem. That's just my directions to your lodge," Dot explained.

"How timely," Mr. Insite said. "That leads us to our next topic. Just as these directions guided you here, a company needs directions to guide its people as they implement the Purpose and the Philosophy. That's where Priorities fit in. Surrounding the organization's Purpose and Philosophy are the Priorities—the values—that further guide its work. Priorities allow people to be self-directed. Individuals can make good choices on their own when they understand the values to abide by. You don't need a lot of rules and regulations. Priorities simplify decision making by setting the critical standards for everyone to follow."

Dot thought about her visit with Mr. Mane. To foster excellence through competition, everyone at Mane Industries demonstrated clear values: aggressiveness, risk taking, innovation and customer service.

Dot asked, "How do you decide your company's Priorities?"

"The Priorities are values important to the leadership. These values must be consistent with your company's Purpose and Philosophy, and they must allow you to be successful in a competitive environment. You don't want a long list of Priorities. Keep it simple with just a few key values that everyone in the organization should follow. Different departments may have additional values that are essential for success in their particular areas, but the Priorities for the organization should be a concise set of values that everyone considers important."

Mr. Insite turned to a blank page in Dot's journal and wrote . . .

INSIGHT # 4

The Priorities of an organization are its key values.

- Priorities guide how the Purpose and the Philosophy are put into practice.

- Priorities are limited to a small number of values appropriate for the whole organization.

- The Priorities are the answer to the question, "What are the most important standards that guide how people do their work?"

Mr. Insite summarized, "You have said that Three Click Express provides the experience of discovery through authentic relationships. What values further guide you in this work?"

"Well, because discovery is our Purpose, it is quite obvious that *learning* is important. One of my favorite quotes is, 'The world is a book, and those who do not travel read only one page.' At Three Click Express, we value learning. Our customers learn through the planning process and, of course, through the travel experience itself. We learn from the relationships we develop and from our research and planning. Expanding the mind is an important part of what we do."

"In addition to learning, what other Priorities guide Three Click Express?" prodded Mr. Insite.

"With a Philosophy that focuses on authentic relationships, our *personalized customer service* Priority is essential. We can't have authentic relationships without it.

"And our caring service is based on *trust*. We value each other's integrity, judgments and opinions. People trust us to provide what they are looking for. Mutual respect and trust are definitely crucial in everything we do.

"And, there's more. We also prioritize *collaboration*, which is consistent with our Philosophy and with our customer service Priority. We work with others in our company as well as with our partners to do the best job for our clients. Plus, we learn more by working together."

Mr. Insite smiled, "I think you understand perfectly,

Dot. You have described a clear set of Priorities: *learning, personalized customer service, trust* and *collaboration.* When you apply these standards consistently at Three Click, you are, indeed, promoting the experience of discovery through authentic relationships.

"Let me further explain," he continued. "Every company has its own set of Priorities. They reflect the Purpose and the Philosophy of the company and its leader. Priorities clearly guide employees' everyday activities. If members' actions support the Priorities, then the company is on its way to great success."

"Is there a right Purpose, Philosophy or set of Priorities that a company should have?" questioned Dot.

"No. An organization, like a person, has a particular nature, a corporate personality. It is important in life to be who you are."

"Once you define a company's Purpose, the Philosophy and the Priorities, do they ever change?" asked Dot.

"It depends," Mr. Insite replied. "Sometimes, even when everyone is clear on the Purpose, the Philosophy and the Priorities, a need may arise to make changes, perhaps to stay competitive. Priorities are key values, but they can be altered as long as the new values are consistent with the Purpose and Philosophy."

"What happens if a company changes its Purpose or Philosophy?" Dot asked.

"Well, let me ask you that question," he proposed. "If either the Purpose or the Philosophy of Three Click changed, what impact would that have on your company?"

"If we were no longer in the business of providing the experience of discovery or if we no longer cared about authentic relationships, it would be quite a different company," responded Dot. "Those are the critical elements that define who we are and, I believe, set us apart from our competitors."

"They are critical," Mr. Insite agreed. "However, a time may come when it is necessary to make a radical change in the Purpose or the Philosophy to stay competitive and survive. Of course, this type of change has a monumental impact on the organization and its members. People who were loyal and committed to the company may feel a loss because the essence of the organization would no longer exist. This often feels like the death of the organization to those who were strongly connected to it. The company may have the same name, but it will feel like a different place. Changing the Purpose or the Philosophy is like founding a new company."

"I know what you mean," Dot said. "People have a hard time dealing with change."

"That's a fact," said Mr. Insite. "Think long and hard before you change either the Purpose or the Philosophy. They are the company's foundation and framework."

"So it looks like it's important to understand and regularly monitor the Purpose, the Philosophy and the Priorities of an organization," Dot said.

"Exactly. They are the very CORE of the organization."

Mr. Insite wrote in Dot's journal . . .

INSIGHT #5

The Purpose, the Philosophy and the Priorities are the CORE Culture of an organization.

- They are the prime beliefs that guide the organization.

- Any change to the Purpose or the Philosophy can have a monumental impact on the organization and its members.

- The Priorities can be altered to keep the organization competitive as long as the new values are consistent with the Purpose and the Philosophy.

"It all comes down to the CORE," Mr. Insite said. "The Purpose, the Philosophy and the Priorities are the CORE Culture of the organization. I call it the CORE Culture because the Purpose, the Philosophy and the Priorities are the central elements of organizational culture. CORE Culture is the substance of your culture and the basis of your company's behavior. It is the total of the prime beliefs and values that guide the entire organization. Everything outside the CORE is just an expression or application of the CORE Culture. The practices that guide members' work, the ways that members interact with others and the approach that the organization uses to project itself to the public are all manifestations of the prime beliefs in the CORE."

Turning to a new page, Mr. Insite continued, "What you have is an easy-to-apply template that a company can use to create its own customized CORE Culture Map."

He drew the familiar three circles and added the words *CORE Culture Map.*

CORE CULTURE MAP

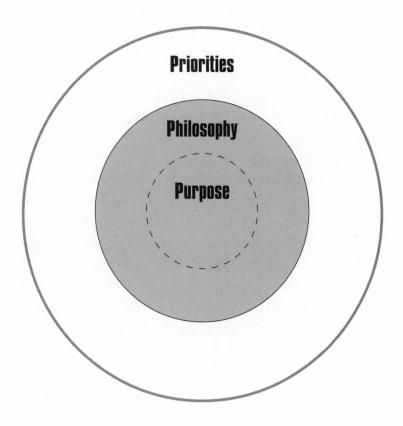

"This is a simple way to chart the principal elements of your company," Mr. Insite continued. "The CORE Culture Map is an important visual. Using this device, everyone has a picture of the organization's key beliefs and values. In my experiences with companies, people have a hard time understanding the concept of workplace culture. The CORE Culture Map is a useful tool because it illustrates and confirms the CORE elements of the culture. It makes a complicated concept clear."

"I agree," Dot said. "I understand things better when they're presented visually."

"People love the clarity of it," he explained. "The CORE Culture Map allows everyone in your organization to speak with the same vocabulary. Having that common language promotes conversation, understanding and collective action. Members of any organization always have a variety of opinions about it. Without an ongoing dialogue, individuals develop varying attitudes and values. The CORE Culture Map identifies the basic principles that people in the organization share."

"I see that now," Dot said.

Mr. Insite added, "When people see these CORE beliefs in black and white, they understand the cultural aspects of the organization that everyone must sustain on an ongoing basis. These must be living principles, an integral part of daily life."

Taking the journal and pen, Dot added to the drawing . . .

THREE CLICK EXPRESS CORE CULTURE MAP

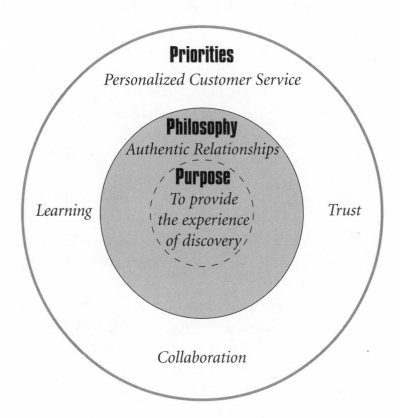

"So, this would be the CORE Culture Map for Three Click Express," Dot stated with confidence.

"You've got it, Dot!" Mr. Insite confirmed emphatically.

"It makes so much sense now," Dot said. "I can't wait to go home to Three Click Express and tell everyone what I've discovered."

"Let me caution you, Dot," advised Mr. Insite. "Going through this process works best when it is an organization-wide activity. Everyone must take part in defining the Purpose, the Philosophy and the Priorities of Three Click Express. When everyone participates in defining these fundamentals, they will feel real ownership of the CORE that unfolds."

"But what if they come up with something different?" Dot asked.

"That's a common concern, but don't worry," he said. "Working together, everyone will see it as it truly is. It always works that way."

"That's reassuring," she said.

"It is absolutely essential for everyone to know the CORE," he clarified. "Everyone must agree with the CORE Culture Map. Bringing people together to define the CORE Culture is an important first step. Then, everyone in your organization must personally connect to the CORE; they must *be* it naturally."

"How does that happen?" Dot wondered.

Mr. Insite explained, "Well, it works two ways: the company must select the right people, and the individual must select the right company. Often a company looks only at an applicant's skills for a particular job, but you need to consider other factors. When selecting people, try to determine whether each individual has a passion for the Purpose, beliefs that support the Philosophy and values that are consistent with the Priorities of your organization. That connection to the CORE Culture promotes loyalty and contributes to the success of the company and the individual."

"And, tell me, how does a person pick the right workplace?" Dot asked. "Sometimes that's not so easy."

"I understand," Mr. Insite acknowledged, "but it is so important for all of us to take responsibility for our own lives. People must be as selective as possible in picking the right organization for them. When you are job hunting, it is best to actively seek a place that fits your beliefs, fulfills your needs and satisfies your dreams. To do this, you must understand yourself as well as the CORE Culture of the organization. And you must choose a company where you can easily connect to and naturally be that CORE. With this awareness, you can determine if a workplace is right for you."

"Once you know and connect to the CORE, is that it?"

"No, that's just the beginning. Then, everyone must work to achieve the CORE," he explained. "Everyone must *do* it, must live it actively. Defining the CORE Culture and building common ground with people who personally support it is only the beginning. This creates *harmony in spirit*. But when everyone works to achieve the CORE, you create *harmony in action.* Everyone must work in ways that support your Purpose, Philosophy and Priorities."

"Is that where the CORE Culture Map comes in?" she asked.

"Yes. The CORE Culture Map serves as a guide," he explained. "People should use it to screen their actions, so they can decide what fits best for the company. You don't need a lot of rules and regulations. Just be consistent with the CORE in the things that you do."

Mr. Insite wrote . . .

INSIGHT # 6

Everyone in an organization must know the CORE, connect to it and work to achieve it.

"It does seem relatively simple now," agreed Dot.

"Precisely," Mr. Insite confirmed.

"Mr. Insite, this has been such a valuable experience for me. I have learned so much," Dot said.

"I'm glad I've been able to help," he responded. "Just be sure to continue the process we have begun."

"I will," Dot said gratefully.

"Remember, Dot, understanding CORE Culture is fundamental. Only then, can you begin the journey toward real success. Everyone must know it, personally connect to it and consistently work to achieve it. Once you've accomplished that, the future can be whatever you envision. That is the path to creating a special kind of workplace."

Mr. Insite turned the page and wrote . . .

INSIGHT #7

**Understanding the CORE is
fundamental to creating
a workplace that is
the right place.**

**Work should be a place
that feels like home.**

"You'll know deep inside when you've found that place," Mr. Insite said as he returned the journal to Dot.

Contemplating his words, Dot slowly turned the pages as she reviewed the seven insights.

THE SEVEN INSIGHTS

INSIGHT #1
**The Purpose of an organization
is the fundamental reason it exists.**

INSIGHT #2
**The Philosophy of an organization
is its distinctiveness.**

INSIGHT #3
**The combination of
the Purpose and the Philosophy is
the identity of an organization.**

INSIGHT #4
**The Priorities of an organization
are its key values.**

INSIGHT #5
**The Purpose, the Philosophy
and the Priorities
are the CORE Culture of an organization.**

INSIGHT #6
**Everyone in an organization must
know the CORE, connect to it
and work to achieve it.**

INSIGHT #7
**Understanding the CORE
is fundamental to creating a workplace
that is the right place.**

Work should be a place that feels like home.

"I do understand," Dot said as she closed the journal and looked once again into the shiny silver cover. "When you create a workplace that feels like home, the CORE of the organization will be a true reflection of who you are. It will possess a Purpose that inspires you, a Philosophy that uniquely defines you and Priorities that you value. It will be a place where you feel comfortable and connected—a workplace where you feel at home.

"And as I have learned," Dot smiled knowingly, "once you discover that, there is no place like work."

AND THE JOURNEY CONTINUES . . .

PART II

Behind the Wizard's Curtain

CHAPTER **6**

A Journey Based on Research

THE CORE Culture strategy is not just an allegory, a fairy tale metaphor or a concept. It is a living, breathing, effective process that has worked for many organizations and that will work for yours.

It began with a significant piece of research—co-author Dr. Sheila L. Margolis's doctoral dissertation—that evolved into a hands-on way to guide your organization through change while nurturing, and not disrupting, the essential elements that make up its identity.

In fact, organizational identity is the topic that Dr. Margolis's research addressed. She was conducting a case study of a company in the commercial airline industry. The firm was undergoing a merger to replace its tarnished image, which had been damaged by intense, unrelenting negative media exposure.

Over a six-month period, Dr. Margolis conducted fifty-two interviews with company employees, observed them in a variety of workplace activities and reviewed countless pages of company-produced print materials as well as articles from local and national newspapers and magazines. She focused on identifying elements of the company that the employees regarded as core, distinctive and enduring.

After extensive information gathering, she analyzed the data and found that a broader picture of organizational attributes emerged. This multifaceted corporate portrait revealed five layers of intrinsic organizational characteristics. Those became the Five Ps: Purpose, Philosophy, Priorities, Practices and Projections.

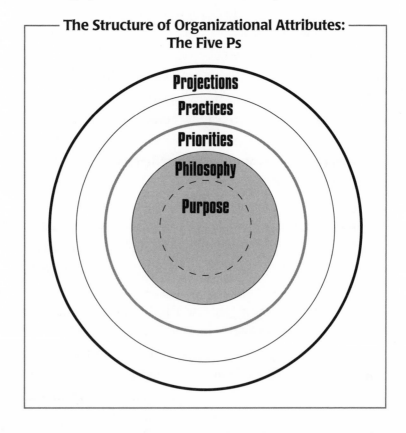

The Structure of Organizational Attributes: The Five Ps

Projections
Practices
Priorities
Philosophy
Purpose

This diagram, which includes the elements of organizational identity as well as the CORE Culture Model, provides a new way to examine an organization, an innovative tool that can guide leaders as they create and build successful, meaningful workplaces.

Crafting consequential theories about human performance in organizations requires research and practice in a variety of organizations. Since this initial study, Dr. Margolis and co-author Dr. Ava S. Wilensky—partners in CORE InSites®, a management consulting firm—have applied the CORE Culture Model's strategic tactics and the Five Ps to help CEOs, managers and employees. During the course of their practice, the goal of creating a meaningful, effective workplace solidified into the concept that a workplace should feel like home. The CORE Culture strategy can show you how to increase the bottom line by building a committed workforce where employees feel a sense of connection and belonging at work.

"There is no place like home," you say? Now you can begin the journey to create a workplace where your employees say, "There is no place like work." Continue your journey down the Yellow Brick Road to learn how to create a more meaningful workplace, thrive with change, build employee morale and increase profits. Take your next step in creating your special workplace: explore the Five Ps.

CHAPTER 7

Minding Your Five Ps

BEFORE you can manage your organization's CORE Culture and build the dedicated workforce you seek, you need a road map of where your culture stands today. That map can be constructed once you understand the five critical intersections, five crucial organizational attributes, the Five Ps: Purpose, Philosophy, Priorities, Practices and Projections.

The first few sections of this chapter provide explanations and cases constructed to enhance your understanding of Purpose, Philosophy and Priorities. After you gain a clear grasp of those CORE Culture elements, a review of the final two Ps—Practices and Projections—follows. Understanding the Five Ps is the starting point for CORE Culture Management. Applying the Five Ps to your organization is the road map for creating a successful workplace. The journey begins with the first of the Five Ps—Purpose.

The Purpose of an Organization

If you think the Purpose of a bakery is just making hot rolls, put your visions of jam and butter aside, and think about the very core of that business. The Purpose is the reason it is important that an organization exists, the cause that defines its contribution to society. This central element of the Five Ps is the heart of your organization: it is what makes work meaningful. To get a better sense of the Purpose, it's time to wake up and smell the aroma of freshly baked bread at a successful regional bakery.

CASE #1: THE BAKERY

The smell of freshly baked bread has the power to transform a rainy afternoon into a Sunday picnic. Customers who walk into the growing regional bakery are instantly wrapped in nostalgic aromas that evoke family celebrations and traditional gatherings. For twenty years, the Bakery has built on its old-world artisan baking techniques to create tantalizing breads and rolls.

When we sat down with these master bakers to discuss their organization's Purpose, we didn't stop with their products. They are not only providing delicious food; they are *nourishing life*—that is their company's Purpose. The Bakery's CEO, the founder of the company, sees their work as continuing a process that has sustained life across civilizations and over thousands of years. From the unleavened bread that crossed the desert with Moses to today's plethora of choices that fill their shelves, the people who work at the Bakery see the production of breads and rolls as vital to the life and health of their customers. With each rise of the dough, all Bakery employees understand their products' beneficial

---

The Bakery CORE Culture Map

Identity: To nourish life with a commitment to high standards

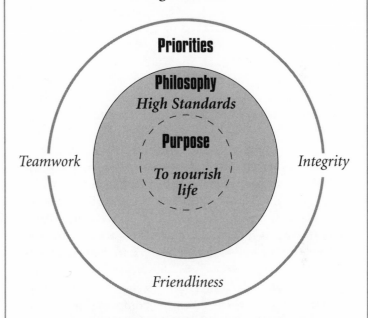

Priorities

Philosophy
High Standards

Purpose

To nourish life

Teamwork

Integrity

Friendliness

How employees describe the Priorities at the Bakery:

Teamwork	Employees work together cooperatively.
Integrity	Every employee is proud to be as reliable and principled as the company itself.
Friendliness	Employees are warm, gracious and responsive.

nature of feeding the body and nourishing the soul. Unified by this elemental Purpose, each person exhibits a genuine dedication to the company and a passion for the work.

The Bakery's Philosophy—a devotion to *high standards*—supports their Purpose. Everyone is passionately committed to providing exceptional baked breads. A rigorous quality assurance program ensures that all products meet or exceed the company's standards prior to distribution. Products must adhere to strict specifications on nutrition, appearance, freshness and taste. Bakers produce their baked goods carefully, without preservatives, following the guild traditions of their European ancestors. This natural process ensures the high quality of each crusty loaf of rye bread, each braided challah, each hot cross bun.

Because professional baking with such high standards is time-consuming and exacting, the Priorities of *teamwork* and *integrity* are essential. Everyone works together cooperatively. Team meetings are held weekly to review processes and find ways to enhance their products. Employees—from the crew of bakers who start at dawn to the front counter staff—are proud to be as reliable and principled as the company itself. They believe in the quality of their products and frequently share information on their production methods and ingredients with their customers. Another Priority is *friendliness*—the company's friendly atmosphere, which encompasses employees and customers. Employees describe their workplace as warm and comfortable. They participate in family picnics and often spend time together outside of work. Because they take a personal pride in their fresh-baked goods, employees are always gracious and responsive with their customers. The

Bakery's culture results in low employee turnover, satisfied customers, healthy profits and an environment that consistently produces delicious baked goods for its growing number of grateful consumers.

Obviously, Purpose doesn't stand alone. It meshes with the Philosophy and the Priorities to form the corporation's CORE Culture. But Purpose comes first. The Bakery's Purpose, *to nourish life,* is a brief and compelling statement of its energizing, heartfelt motivation. To find your organization's Purpose, ask yourself, and the people who work with you, why the organization exists. What is its reason for being?

Your employees need to have a sense of the organization's Purpose. When members know how their daily activities contribute to the Purpose, they feel a part of a larger and more significant effort. Think back to Dot's visit to Heartland Pharmaceuticals, where the Purpose is not limited to just making medications, but defined with a broader scope—to preserve and enhance life. Such a Purpose allows members to view their work through a wider filter that expands their outlook and their possibilities and enables them to build an enduring organization. The Purpose is the central cause that makes your work meaningful.

Some examples of Purpose statements are listed in the chart below.

General Examples of Purpose

Organization	Purpose
Bank	To help people achieve their dreams
Chemical company	To improve living environments
Entertainment company	To make people happy
Hospitality association	To provide a united voice for the hospitality industry
Internet company	To connect people to power and possibilities
Physician group	To preserve health and patient well-being

The next chart presents additional examples from well-known organizations to help you better understand this essential element.

Specific Examples of Purpose

Organization	Purpose
Bear Stearns	To build value
Best Buy	To make life fun and easy
Blue-Cross Blue-Shield of Tennessee	To provide peace of mind
CARE	To reduce poverty
The Carter Center	To advance human rights and alleviate unnecessary human suffering
Cingular Wireless	To provide wireless technology designed to enrich lives
The Coca-Cola Company	To benefit and refresh everyone it touches
General Electric Company	To solve problems
Google	To organize the world's information and make it universally accessible and useful
SYSCO	To help our customers succeed
VIACOM	To inform and entertain
Women's Business Enterprise National Council	To advance the success of women's enterprises

The Purpose is the central feature in the structure of the Five Ps and the foundation for all other organizational attributes. Yet, by itself, the Purpose does not constitute the entirety of a company's CORE identity. The Purpose is essential and enduring but rarely distinctive. Now it needs marching orders.

The Philosophy of an Organization

The second essential feature that completes the definition of organizational identity is the Philosophy, the Purpose's essential companion. The Purpose is the foundation that defines why the organization exists, but the Philosophy is the vital framework for how members do that work.

The Philosophy, as illustrated by I.Q. at Intellitoy, specifies the central character of the company, the single element that members believe is fundamental, positive and distinctive—the factor that has set the company apart from its competitors over the years. At Intellitoy, the Philosophy is intelligence. At the Bakery, it is high standards.

The Philosophy will vary based on an organization's nature and the ethos of its founder. The founder's personality and skills or the ideals that drove the organization's creation often emerge as the organization's Philosophy.

The Philosophy is not just any value—it is the prime value that guides the organization and has a dominant impact on how employees perform their work. The Philosophy can be subtle and difficult to define, but consider these descriptions of what a culture-shaping Philosophy looks like in action.

Descriptions of Philosophy

- *Customer service*—The members of this Internet company don't just care about customer service, they obsess over it. Customer service is vital to who they are and everything they do. They measure it, they constantly implement programs to enhance it and they talk about it all the time. Everything in the company hinges on bringing value to the customer, whether through low prices, an impressive array of products or a convenient buying process. The company gives customers a wealth of information to help them make the best buying decisions. The firm's continual upgrades in processes and features are driven by the goal of serving the customer in a distinctive way. Its competitors don't even come close.

- *Family orientation*—This mid-size manufacturing and sales organization is governed by its unique family-oriented Philosophy. The founder started the company as a family business and created an organization built on a prime personal value: the importance of people. Today's leadership, now the third generation, still feels genuine concern about employees' growth, careers and happiness. Members see the company as a safe haven where they share a special camaraderie and take care of each other. That family Philosophy extends to customers through the employees' focus on relationships and the personal interest that they take in each individual. The company's leaders and its members view its family-oriented Philosophy as the key to their success.

- *Innovation*—The Philosophy of a premier high-tech company is innovation. The founder sees innovation as the key to providing technology-based solutions for its customers. Managers trust that innovation comes from unexpected events and the individual initiatives of imaginative and industrious employees. The leadership maintains a culture of openness to new ideas, support for collaboration and commitment to research and development. The organization's unique innovative culture is the bedrock of its priceless reputation in its field.

- *Control*—This logistics firm has an autocratic leader who believes in executive control and absolute precision. This founder holds tight reins over the organization, requiring employees to adhere to a strict chain of command. The clear hierarchy cannot be violated, leaving individuals with limited authority but defined tasks. The leadership values loyalty and provides incentive pay based on individual performance. Employees enjoy a nine-to-five job with definite parameters and specified responsibilities.

- *Massiveness*—This large national sales organization views its very size as its Philosophy. The leaders and employees see the tremendous breadth of their company as their distinctiveness. The organization has more products, more sales reps, more markets, more trucks and more customers than any other company in its industry. Their size enables them to succeed in a very competitive, low-margin business. The members are proud to work for the largest company in the industry, and the company's Philosophy makes them feel as big as it is.

Your company's Philosophy is its root value. It is the organizing principle guiding the way you conduct your business.

Organizational Identity:
Uniting Purpose and Philosophy

As a unit, the Purpose and the Philosophy constitute organizational identity: the enduring essence of an organization, the core that differentiates it from all others. These stable identity elements are a unique product of the organization's history, not something that can be copied from others. They must be authentic.

The Purpose and the Philosophy are a source of competitive advantage and the basis and anchor for behaviors and actions. They define how issues are viewed and evoke predictable emotions from insiders. The Purpose and the Philosophy together are the central and distinctive attributes of your organization, the intrinsic nature that, most likely, has remained highly resistant to change over the years.

You have read about the organizational identity of several companies on Dot's journey to Reflection City: the identity of Intellitoy is to promote fun with a focus on intelligence; the identity of Mane Industries is to promote excellence with a relentless appetite for competition; and of course, the identity of Three Click Express is to provide the experience of discovery through authentic relationships. These identity statements capture the enduring foundation and framework for each organization.

The Priorities of an Organization

In the map of the Five Ps, the Priorities are located immediately outside of the Purpose and the Philosophy. They are the third component of CORE Culture, yet not a part of organizational identity. The Priorities are the organization's core values that support the Purpose and the Philosophy. Don't confuse the Priorities with the organization's Philosophy. The Philosophy is the prime value that is central to the organization; it is both distinctive and enduring. The Priorities are supporting values that guide the organization in living its Purpose and Philosophy. The Priorities are not as central to the organization as the Philosophy, and they do not have to be either distinctive or enduring. Although Priorities are relatively stable, you can change these values, when necessary, to enhance your organization's Purpose or Philosophy and make it more competitive. The powerful pairing of Purpose and Philosophy supported by the Priorities can be demonstrated in the nonprofit sector as well as the for-profit world.

CASE #2: THE ADDICTION TREATMENT CENTER

The Addiction Treatment Center has provided residential and outpatient addiction services for a metropolitan inner city for more than thirty years. Its Purpose is straightforward: *to rebuild lives,* but that is carried out within the context of its Philosophy of *quality.*

The organization offers a broad scope of comprehensive, high-quality treatment and recovery services

The Addiction Treatment Center
CORE Culture Map

*Identity: To rebuild lives with a distinctive
dedication to quality*

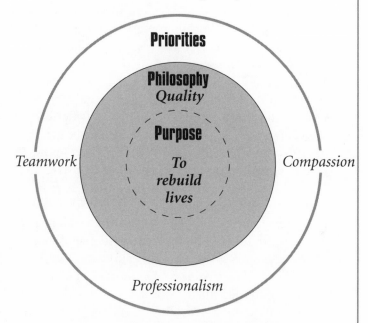

How employees describe the Priorities
at the Addiction Treatment Center:

Teamwork	Employees work together, helping and advising each other.
Compassion	Employees genuinely care about each other and the people they serve.
Professionalism	The center has a nationally ranked medical staff, the facility has various accreditations and employees conduct business in a professional manner.

for people who are addicted to drugs or alcohol. It reaches out to all ages, ethnic groups and social classes. The center demonstrates its focus on quality through its people and its services. The staff is highly credentialed and well trained, the management is dedicated and focused and the board is single-mindedly committed to providing the funding to carry out the organization's work. The services exceed the highest standards, with extras such as translators who are fluent in the many languages a big city base requires and social workers who provide individualized follow up to guide people through the transition back into the outside world. The center, with its 90 percent success rate, is fairly touted as the best facility of its kind in the country.

Since we are discussing Priorities, consider the center's key values: *teamwork, compassion* and *professionalism*. The importance placed on *teamwork* is apparent from the way everyone works together, helping and advising each other as they address their clients' needs case by case in order to provide quality care. Members are known for Prioritizing *compassion*. Their ability to be tough and empathetic is a key combination that builds positive results. Members genuinely care about each other and the people they serve. And the nationally ranked medical staff, the facility's various accreditations and the way they conduct business all demonstrate *professionalism*. These Priorities enable members to deliver quality services that change lives.

You've read about other Priorities on Dot's journey: the Priorities of Mane Industries are aggressiveness, risk taking, innovation and customer service; and the Priorities of Three

Click Express are learning, personalized customer service, trust and collaboration. In addition, at the Bakery the Priorities are teamwork, integrity and friendliness. And as you've just learned at the Addiction Treatment Center, the Priorities are teamwork, compassion and professionalism.

Many of these Priorities may "sound good," but that is not the criteria for selecting the ones that belong on your organization's CORE Culture Map. The key is for you to identify those few Priorities that, if followed by everyone in your organization, would effectively support the Purpose and the Philosophy and would enable the organization to achieve its goals.

Many Priorities are similar in nature as you see by the examples below.

Selected Priorities by Theme

Theme	Priorities
If an organization values:	The Priority may be expressed as:
People	Caring, Compassion, Relationships, Personalization, Friendliness
Working Together	Teamwork, Collaboration, Partnerships, Collegiality, Cooperation
Being Smart	Talent, Intelligence, Learning, Knowledge
Time	Efficiency, Speed, Sense of Urgency, Nimbleness
Determination	Aggressiveness, Hard Work, Drive, Perseverance
Originality	Innovation, Creativity, Imagination, Inventiveness
Ethics	Integrity, Honesty, Trust, Transparency

Values can seem comparable in definition but be different in tone. For example, the Bakery uses *friendliness* to describe a key value of their organization rather than other similar values like caring, compassion, relationships or personalization. The Bakery believes *friendliness* is a more descriptive key value of their organization. At the Addiction Treatment Center, members value the Priority of *teamwork*; they believe that this Priority is more representative of their organization than other related values such as collaboration, partnerships, collegiality and cooperation. As these cases illustrate, select the Priorities that define what matters most to your organization and target the nuance of what it intends to accomplish.

Don't make a long list of Priorities. Limit your organization's Priority agenda to the most important values that every employee is committed to fulfilling. Some values are important to one arm of the organization and not the other; save those values for departmental strategizing. Your organization-wide CORE Culture Map should only include Priorities that are appropriate for the whole organization.

The Priorities support the Purpose and the Philosophy, and they help set the standards for how work gets accomplished. When employees have to make decisions, the Priorities give them guidelines to follow.

CORE Culture:
The Purpose, the Philosophy and the Priorities

The central three Ps—the Purpose, the Philosophy and the Priorities—constitute the CORE Culture of the organization. Let's examine how these elements blend together to form a successful university.

CASE #3: THE UNIVERSITY

In the early 1900s, an evening-school program at a prominent university evolved into a small, independent college. Now, almost one hundred years later, the University is an independent, dynamic academic institution, offering graduate and undergraduate degrees in numerous fields of study.

Located in the downtown business district of a large metropolitan city, the University has defined its Purpose as *being a source of limitless potential.* It seeks to support individual development and the improvement of society. Because of its urban setting, the University has a real commitment to the city. The University's president feels strongly that its *urban* character contributes to the school's distinctiveness. This Philosophy focuses not only on meeting students' needs, but also on serving people in the surrounding businesses and neighborhoods. The University takes pride in its cosmopolitan image, its strong presence in the downtown area and its innovative, service-based curriculum. Students and professors alike view the city as an extension of their campus and an opportunity for contribution.

The University's Priority of *diversity* supports the way it nurtures, understands and supports students from all fifty states and from more than a hundred

The University CORE Culture Map

Identity: To be a source of limitless potential driven by an urban focus

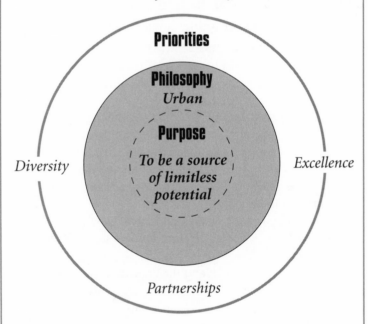

How employees describe the Priorities at the University:

Diversity — The University provides educational opportunities for nontraditional and traditional students from nearly every cultural, ethnic, religious and racial background.

Excellence — The University has exceptional faculty members and strong academic programs.

Partnerships — The University fosters collaborative relations with businesses, nonprofits, other educational institutions and local governments.

other countries. The University takes pride in providing educational opportunities for nontraditional and traditional students from nearly every cultural, ethnic, religious and racial background. The University carries out its Priority of *excellence* by hiring exceptional faculty members who are widely respected in their fields and by building strong academic programs. It lives its Priority of building *partnerships* by fostering collaborative relationships with businesses, nonprofits, other educational institutions and local governments. For an urban University, building partnerships is good business and the city setting is a laboratory for learning. These values—diversity, excellence and partnerships—clearly sustain the University's Purpose and Philosophy and create a system where teaching, research and public service flow freely between the school and community it serves.

The CORE Culture is the cluster of organizational principles that serve as the basis for action. Although Priorities can change when necessary, CORE Culture is fairly stable. When you examine two organizations in the same field or industry, you will find that variances in CORE Culture form the basis for the distinctions between them.

You may also notice that a Priority in one organization may be a Philosophy in another. For example, *relationships* is the prime value or Philosophy at Three Click Express, but, as you will see in the next case of the Communications Company, *relationships* is one of three supporting values and thus a Priority.

CASE #4:
THE COMMUNICATIONS COMPANY

For the first ten years of its existence, this network communications company was involved in entertainment production. But, like many companies, it sought change, and new partners joined the management. The partners were eager to explore fresh ways to expand the company's creativity and profit potential. They decided to broaden the company's scope from entertainment production to media and message management. They changed the company's name, positioned it as a provider of communications strategy and defined its Purpose: *to enhance image.*

Now a leading provider of communications services, the company promises its clients positive business and personal results from media exposure. Because the partners have extensive on-air network knowledge and top-notch journalism, editorial and production expertise, they define *talent* as their Philosophy—the distinctive feature of their organization. Building the firm's high-level corporate- and entertainment-world client list requires hiring people with experience and name recognition. The company hires multitalented people with media-business connections and image-building expertise, with knowledge ranging from how to pitch stories to how to make perfect videos.

The company's first Priority is *excellence.* With a Philosophy focused on talent, the Priority of excellent work is a natural. The company believes in providing the best, high-quality services, crafting clients' messages for maximum impact. But, being deeply knowledgeable of how quickly people who live in the media spotlight burn out, they also adopted the Priority of a healthy *work-life*

The Communications Company
CORE Culture Map

Identity: To enhance image through exceptional talent

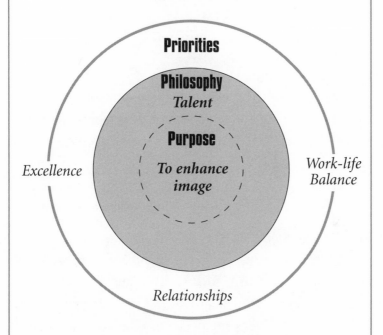

How employees describe the Priorities at the Communications Company:

Excellence	The company provides the best, high-quality services, crafting clients' messages for maximum impact.
Work-life Balance	The company strives to create a kinder, gentler workplace.
Relationships	Employees deeply understand and support each person's ability to contribute.

balance. They feel passionate about creating a kinder, gentler workplace that allows flexibility as long as the job gets done. The company also has a people focus, as demonstrated by the Priority on *relationships.* Working as a team of talented professionals, they deeply understand and support each person's ability to contribute to the company's success. Their focus on relationships with their clients allows them to provide superb work through customized service, grounded in strong and sincere relationships.

The three CORE elements—the Purpose, the Philosophy and the Priorities—when woven tightly together, make your organization unique. These three Ps are fundamental to the organization and govern all aspects of work.

The Practices of an Organization

Before you consider your organization's Practices, take another look at CORE Culture and the remaining layers of organizational attributes as illustrated in the Five Ps. The Practices are located immediately outside of the CORE Culture for a reason: they are not the elements of CORE Culture, but they do carry it out. Here's where the rubber meets the road.

Practices are either internal or external, within your company or on the street amid the rough and tumble of suppliers and customers.

Note the placement of Internal and External Practices within the five Ps.

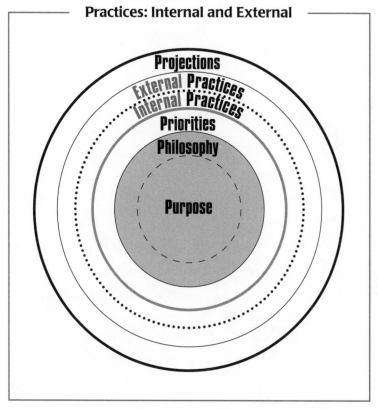

Practices: Internal and External

Be sure to infuse your CORE Culture principles and values into the internal workings of your organization. Internal Practices affect employee relationships, interactions and accomplishments. These Practices cover your company's structure, systems and processes as illustrated by the categories on the next page.

Internal Practices Categories

- *Organizational structure and work design practices*—Pay attention to your reporting structure, specific roles and responsibilities and workflow.

- *Employment practices*—Provide guidelines for recruiting and hiring the right people for your company.

- *Training and development practices*—Offer individual or group learning and development activities that help your employees assess their strengths and weaknesses, build on their strengths and improve their ability to contribute.

- *Performance management practices*—Improve performance by defining individual tasks and goals. Be sure to establish performance standards; measure, monitor and evaluate individual progress; design a plan to promote individual development; celebrate success; provide performance-based compensation; and promote succession planning.

- *Internal communications practices*—Develop formal and informal procedures for two-way information sharing so everyone effectively sends and receives information.

- *Technology practices*—Facilitate work to make the organization more efficient and productive. Support your employees by providing the most accurate data and the most effective equipment.

A company also has External Practices that define how your organization interacts with outsiders—those who are not employees. The External Practices categories on the next page must be in line with your CORE Culture.

External Practices Categories

- *Customers*—Target customer and market segments where you will best compete. Cement relationships with your customers through shared values. Use the passion that drives you to build a loyal, profitable and delighted customer base.

- *Products and Services*—Reflect on the products and services that you offer and the programs and services you provide. Ensure that the traits that make you special are apparent in what you do. Let your energy be guided by your Purpose and create products and services that highlight your distinctive edge.

- *Suppliers and Vendors*—Screen your suppliers for more than just capability. Consider cultural traits that could cause conflict. Motivate productive partnerships through aligned interests and objectives. Manage and measure performance against the values that matter most to you.

To preserve meaning, motivation and authenticity, make sure that your organization's Internal and External Practices reflect its CORE Culture: its Purpose, Philosophy and Priorities. Don't state that your Priority is work-life balance and then make people come in every weekend. Don't assert that your Philosophy is excellence if you buy knockoff materials. Say—and be—who you really are, internally and externally.

The Projections of an Organization

You've made it to the outer rim—the final P in the Five Ps: the Projections. These are the attributes that display the organization's image to the public, letting them know what you do and why and how you do it. What you project through your publications and public relations are not the substance of your organization's CORE Culture; instead they are reflections of that CORE.

Some ways organizations reflect their image to the public are listed in the following chart.

Projections Categories

- *The name of your company*
- *Your company's logo and other corporate symbols*
- *The location of your corporate headquarters*
- *Your image as a leader of the company*
- *The design and appearance of your offices or stores*
- *Your employees' manner of dress or uniforms*
- *Your marketing, public relations and advertising*
- *Your community activities*

Projections are not the guts of the organization, but they are its portrait. Your image is not only illuminating to the public, but also significant to your members. Dedicated employees feel a lot of emotional attachment to certain Projections, such as the company's name and logo or its reputation for quality or public service because these symbols and statements embody the organization's CORE attributes.

CHAPTER 8

Managing Your CORE Culture Using the Five Ps

THE Bakery always pays attention to high standards. The Addiction Treatment Center stays on the cutting edge of drug and alcohol interventions. The University constantly monitors its urban presence and contribution. And the Communications Company is always the first to recruit well-known, experienced television anchors, so that it can remain on the front lines of top talent and contacts. Each organization is paying continuous attention to its CORE Culture.

With an understanding of the Five Ps, you can embark on the road of CORE Culture Management. The heart of CORE Culture Management is keeping an ongoing watch on every facet of your organization's activities to carry out, intensify and preserve your CORE Culture.

Knowing Your CORE Culture

To begin the process, first make sure that everyone in your organization views the key elements of your CORE Culture similarly. This collective understanding is absolutely crucial. If members do not share these CORE Culture

principles and values, they may act in ways that contra-
dict, distort or damage the organization's CORE Culture
and defeat its objectives.

Define your CORE Culture elements by creating an
organization-wide experience that forcefully brings the
importance of culture to the forefront of members' thinking
and sets the stage to create and confirm a shared view.

Initially, your Purpose, Philosophy and Priorities
may not be apparent to your members or, depending on
where you are in this process, even to you. But they will
emerge as you ask members what they think your organization's CORE really is. We've provided a tool for this
activity in Chapter 9, which lists provocative interview
or focus group questions you can use to delve into your
perceptions and the views of organizational members as
you evolve a mutual set of Purpose, Philosophy and
Priority statements.

Compile answers to these probing questions to build
an overall understanding of the importance of your organization's activities and the values that guide them. You
can also use surveys to gather information or confirm
member beliefs. Once you develop a Purpose statement, a
Philosophy and a set of Priorities that members affirm,
create a CORE Culture Map as a visual cue and use it as a
mechanism for communicating your organization's central concepts, as identified by its members.

The Secret Path to CORE Culture Management: Alignment

Once members clearly understand the CORE Culture, you must create an atmosphere that aligns everyone's actions to it. This is where the Practices and Projections come in.

As the leader, make sure that everyone feels responsibility as a culture manager to act in ways that maintain the CORE Culture and make it even more vibrant. When members' actions support and reinforce your organization's CORE Culture, the organization will have a sense of unshakable stability, even when it experiences change or market upheaval.

All members should work to sustain the CORE. Don't leave anyone out, at any level of the company, to avoid fragmenting the effort and undermining the CORE. As you know, various functional groups or levels within an organization act as subcultures, so departments or work groups may have their own perspectives about their jobs. This internal variety is a positive factor, as long as everyone shares, supports and appreciates the CORE Culture.

Think about the various types of Practices in your organization. Your Internal Practices as well as your External Practices must be considered and aligned with the CORE Culture to build unity, meaning and stability.

Some Internal Practices are particularly crucial to making this happen. For example, it is important to effectively interview and hire people who naturally and genuinely align with your organization's primary values. Someone whose personal mindset is consistent with your CORE Culture is intrinsically motivated to act productively in the light of that culture. When the members of your organization feel personally connected to its Purpose, Philosophy and Priorities, they will work to achieve them more readily. A member's connection to your CORE Culture is cognitive as well as emotional. This powerful unity in spirit can create a self-fulfilling overall belief in the organization's destiny.

The chart on the following pages gives a few examples of the alignment of Internal Practices to an element of a company's CORE Culture. As the chart illustrates, Georgia Pacific values safety and incorporates that Priority in its training and development. IBM applies innovation to how its employees share information. Starbucks demonstrates the value of diversity in its selection practices. And Yahoo! uses fun to celebrate success.

Alignment with CORE Culture: Internal Practices

Company: Georgia Pacific	
CORE Culture Element	**Internal Practice Example**
Safety:	**Training and Development:**
The safety of our employees, the environment and the communities where we operate is our first priority. There is no job so important that it cannot be done safely. Always "do what's right."	We take great pride in our ranking as the safest company in the forest products industry. We are so serious about safety that we have been named the safest forest products company in the industry seven years in a row. Anything less is unacceptable. To promote health and safety awareness, Georgia Pacific's Wauna, Oregon, consumer products mill hosted its third annual Health & Safety Fair last summer. More than one thousand employees, family members and Georgia Pacific retirees attended.

Company: IBM	
CORE Culture Element	**Internal Practice Example**
Innovation:	**Internal Communications:**
Innovation that matters—for our company and for the world.	The New Ideas Program—we have reinvented the employee suggestion system for a more collaborative era, enabling and incenting employees to brainstorm online and work together to refine ideas for productivity improvements.

Alignment with CORE Culture: Internal Practices

Company: Starbucks

CORE Culture Element	Internal Practice Example
Diversity: To embrace diversity as an essential component in the way we do business.	**Employment Practices— Selection:** More than 60 percent of our total workforce is comprised of minorities and/or women. We actively recruit from job fairs focused on minorities, women and people with disabilities.

Company: Yahoo!

CORE Culture Element	Internal Practice Example
Fun: We believe humor is essential to success. We applaud irreverence and don't take ourselves too seriously. We celebrate achievement. We yodel.	**Performance Management:** What better way to start off the New Year than to celebrate each other's successes and rally for the hard work ahead? Our Quarterly All Hands Meetings and live global webcasts allow us to get the entire team together, share information, ask questions and give each other a big round of applause.

Successful companies also ensure that their External Practices reinforce the CORE elements that they value. The J. M. Smucker Company's prime value of quality is practiced by the high-quality products that it sells. Patcraft demonstrates its focus on integrity in its honest and straightforward interactions with customers. Wal-Mart lives its value of service to customers by delivering aggressive hospitality. Whole Foods Market requires that its standard for high quality is also applied to its external suppliers and vendors. The following chart provides these examples.

Alignment with CORE Culture: External Practices

Company: The J. M. Smucker Company

CORE Culture Element	External Practice Example
Quality: Quality applies to our products, our manufacturing methods, our marketing efforts, our people and our relationships with each other. We only produce and sell products that enhance the quality of life and well-being.	**Products:** These will be the highest-quality products offered in our respective markets because the company's growth and business success have been built on quality.

Company: PATCRAFT (a division of Shaw Industries)

CORE Culture Element	External Practice Example
Integrity: Ethical, high-integrity approach to doing business.	**Services:** Our customers trust that we will supply them with the best service possible. We are straightforward, live up to our commitments and stand behind what we say.

Alignment with CORE Culture: External Practices

Company: Wal-Mart

CORE Culture Element	External Practice Example
Service to Our Customers: We want our customers to trust in our pricing philosophy and to always be able to find the lowest prices with the best possible service. We're nothing without our customers.	**Services:** Years ago, Sam Walton challenged all Wal-Mart associates to practice what he called "aggressive hospitality." He said, "Let's be the most friendly—offer a smile of welcome and assistance to all who do us a favor by entering our stores. Give better service—over and beyond what our customers expect. Why not? You wonderful, caring associates can do it and do it better than any other retailing company in the world . . . exceed your customers' expectations. If you do, they'll come back over and over again."

Company: Whole Foods Market

CORE Culture Element	External Practice Example
Selling the Highest-Quality Natural and Organic Products Available: We have high standards, and our goal is to sell the highest-quality products we possibly can. We are the buying agents for our customers and not the selling agents for the manufacturers. Healthy foods and healthy products begin at the source.	**Suppliers/Vendors:** We are advocates and supporters of naturally raised meat and poultry. We work with ranchers and producers to develop hormone and antibiotic-free alternatives for our customers to buy. Producers in the Whole Foods Market natural meat program are visited by the company's meat experts to verify raising and handling practices.

You must also align the Projections of your organization with the CORE Culture. For example, think about your organization's marketing efforts. Do they reflect and reinforce elements of the organization's CORE? Be sure that the images that you project are honest reflections of who you are. Images are easy to manipulate, but they must be grounded in substance. Seek true harmony between your internal identity and your externally presented portrait. This fosters realistic perceptions that are consistent with your organization's nature.

The next chart provides examples of the alignment of a company's Projections to an element of its CORE Culture. BP shares with the public its concern for the environment through its advertising. Dell promotes its focus on direct relationships through its Dell Direct Stores. Levi Strauss & Co. projects its value of originality through innovative marketing. And UPS demonstrates its focus on quality through its valued corporate symbols and tagline.

Alignment with CORE Culture: Projections

Company: BP

CORE Culture Element	Projection Example
Health, Safety and Environment— Environmentally Sound Operations: To conduct the group's activities in a manner that, consistent with the board goals, is environmentally responsible with the aspiration of "no damage to the environment." The group will seek to drive down the environmental impact of its operations by reducing waste, emissions and discharges, and by using energy efficiently.	**Advertising copy:** Environment—To provide heat, power and mobility for the United States, new pipelines have to be built. In Louisiana, BP pioneered a new standard for pipeline construction. Working with environmental groups, community leaders, even local oystermen, we produced a solution that preserved wetlands.

Company: Dell

CORE Culture Element	Projection Example
Direct Relationships: We believe strongly in treating people—customers, partners, suppliers and each other—fairly, openly and respectfully.	**Offices/Stores:** Visit a Dell Direct Store to experience the latest Dell desktops, notebooks, LCD Televisions and Digital Jukeboxes live and in person. You can talk to a Dell expert face-to-face to find the perfect Dell PC, LCD TV or Digital Jukebox for you, order it, and have it shipped right to your home!

Alignment with CORE Culture: Projections

Company: Levi Strauss & Co.

CORE Culture Element	Projection Example
Originality–Being Authentic and Innovative: Levi Strauss started the company and forever earned a place in history. Today, the Levi's® brand is an authentic American icon, known the world over. Innovation is the hallmark of our history. It started with Levi's® jeans, but that pioneering spirit permeates all aspects of our business.	**Marketing:** We were the first U.S. apparel company to use radio and television to market our products.

Company: UPS

CORE Culture Element	Projection Example
Quality: For decades, UPS people have been motivated by commonly held principles and values that have allowed us to work toward mutual goals. These principles and values, originally established by our founders, remain as constant and as critical to our success as ever. The core of these values, which still inspires UPS employees today, is that UPS is a company of honesty, quality and integrity.	**Logo (color and symbol):** Throughout history there have been different symbols, images and logos that have come to symbolize UPS, but one thing always remains the same . . . the color brown and the UPS shield are synonymous with quality service. **Tagline:** "What can brown do for you?"

Evaluate all of your organization's Practices and Projections based on their alignment with the CORE. This consistency shows members and the public that your organization is sincere about its Purpose, Philosophy and Priorities as reflected in the way it acts every day.

Measuring Your Achievements

While aligning your Practices and Projections to your CORE Culture, you also need to position the organization to achieve its strategy. Participants must understand the organization's future direction, so they can focus their individual actions effectively. To help members work more consciously to achieve success, everyone in your organization must be able to objectively measure their contribution to accomplishing desired goals.

Strategy requires a guiding vision and specific, quantifiable strategic goals, backed by action plans for executing the tasks necessary to achieve those goals. Base your strategy on a realistic view of your organization, its environment and its CORE Culture. State strategic goals clearly and make them measurable so you can monitor your organization's progress.

Every member must remain continuously aware of aligning the Practices and Projections not only to the Purpose, the Philosophy and the Priorities, but also to the agreed-upon strategy. All activities must be in sync with who the organization is and where it seeks to go. This dual focus—on CORE Culture and strategy—builds stability and long-term capability.

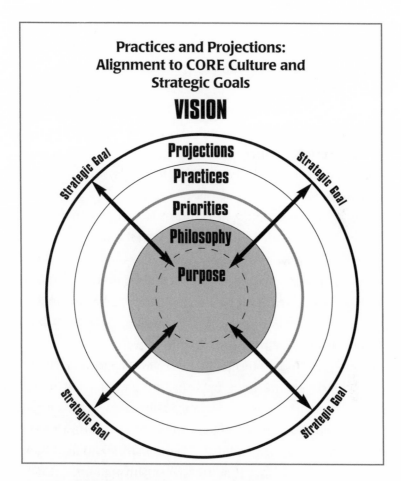

Practices and Projections:
Alignment to CORE Culture and
Strategic Goals

VISION

Projections
Practices
Priorities
Philosophy
Purpose

Strategic Goal
Strategic Goal
Strategic Goal
Strategic Goal

CORE Culture and Managing Change

Elements of CORE Culture are most vulnerable during mergers, acquisitions, market shifts, leadership changes and the advent of new strategies. Often, leaders who do not understand CORE Culture Management or do not want to sustain the current culture will alter the organization's very essence—the Purpose and the Philosophy at the bedrock of its CORE Culture. This can have an extremely negative impact on members who are connected to those identity elements and committed to preserving those prime beliefs.

Changes in the organization's Purpose and Philosophy have the power to stir up emotions and produce feelings of loss, uncertainty, anger and helplessness. People may fear that they are losing the connection to their workplace—the environment they depend upon—because they personally relate to those identity attributes and are committed to them. When leaders tamper with the Purpose or the Philosophy or when systemic change does not confirm the sustainability of these organization-defining elements, people feel as if their treasured past is being stripped away. This is not a recipe for building a dedicated and motivated workforce. This is a recipe for turnover and trouble.

Internal and External Practices are open to change, particularly in the light of your company's need to be competitive. However, remember alignment. Any change in Internal Practices can have either a positive or a negative impact on how employees do their work and how they feel about it. If new Practices filter through the CORE Culture and move the organization strategically ahead, members will typically view the change as positive—even though change itself is always a challenge. If the change contradicts the CORE Culture, you are asking for dissatisfaction, disillusionment and discontent.

Leaders often manipulate projected images to influence public perception for the company's benefit. But to offer a genuine image to the public, you must link that image to your organization's CORE Culture.

Inevitably, throughout the life of an organization, many of its attributes will be eliminated or modified. Even Priorities can be altered, if necessary, to be competitive. As long as the changes continue to support the Purpose and the Philosophy and enable the organization to achieve its strategy, members will usually accept them.

As a leader, remember the importance of communicating with employees about new Priorities, Practices and Projections. Be sure to explain how these changes align with your organization's Purpose and Philosophy while positioning it to achieve its business strategy.

During change, the Purpose and the Philosophy are not fluid. They are the shared attributes that preserve your members' collective mindset. Preserving the Purpose and the Philosophy during change gives members a sense of stability. If you drop or significantly alter the Purpose or the Philosophy, your members will come to view your organization as a different entity—and that can sever their sense of connection.

All leaders know that dramatic change is sometimes necessary or even essential for an organization's survival. In such crises, leaders must actively explain to members the need for change and must communicate a vision for a new future. Done effectively, this will position members to understand and more likely support change. Those who are committed to the present CORE Culture will still see the company as a different organization, but with up-front candor you can empower them to reevaluate their loyalty to it based on the change. Some will be able to connect to the new vision and the altered CORE. However, those who find that the shifted CORE Culture no longer resonates with them may also determine that the company no longer feels like home. That is the risk you take as a leader.

Pay ongoing attention to CORE Culture Management, using the CORE Culture Map as your focal point for analysis and action. Manage your organization's culture to build continuity and united focus. With this strong foundation and framework for organizational success and with clarity in your strategic outlook, your members can achieve their unlimited potential and so can your company.

CHAPTER 9

A CORE Culture Interview Guide

TO begin the process of determining your organization's CORE Culture, stop and reflect on the questions below. Your responses will uncover your view of the Purpose, the Philosophy and the Priorities. To create the CORE Culture Map that everyone shares, all members must participate through interviews, focus groups or surveys. Once you develop a Purpose statement, a Philosophy and a set of Priorities that members affirm, you may record your findings on the CORE Culture Map provided at the end of the chapter.

[Initial CORE Culture Perceptions]
1. When you think of this organization, what words would you use to describe it? Think about ways that the organization demonstrates these traits.

[Purpose]
2. What is the Purpose of this organization?
3. Why is this work important? (Ask this question several times to get to the real Purpose.)

[Philosophy]
4. What primary attribute makes this organization different, special and distinctive from other organizations in the same business?
5. Describe the founder of this organization. What special attributes does/did the founder possess that have influenced the organization's character?

[Purpose, Philosophy or Priorities]
6. What special attribute does the current leader (if the current leader is not the founder) possess?
7. What attribute does the organization emphasize the most? Describe an example of it in practice.

[Priorities]
8. What values are important in this organization? Describe examples of each value in action.
9. What are the important standards that guide how people do their work?

[Purpose and Philosophy]
10. If you had been asked these questions two years ago, would you have used the same words or different ones to describe this organization? (Think through all of the above answers and decide which responses have passed the test of time.)
11. Do you expect the description of this organization today to be the same two years from now? If not, what do you think will change?

CORE CULTURE MAP

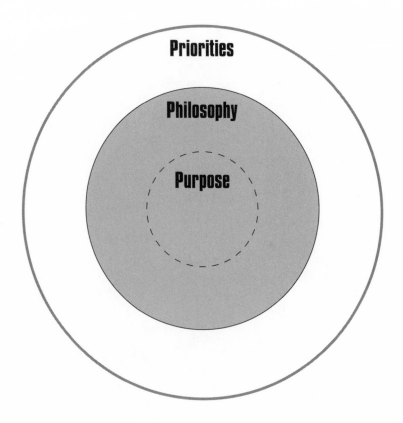

ACKNOWLEDGMENTS

THERE are many people we would like to thank for their contributions to the creation of this book. Their wisdom and insight provided the map for our journey.

To our friends and supporters—Roger Baum, Dennis Berry, Patty and Larry Brown, Bob Chandler, Gail Evans, Donna and Mark Fleishman, Carol Hansen, Gail and Lyons Heyman, Michael Leven, Debbie Levy, Joel Marks, Harry Maziar, JacLynn Morris, Judy Paul, Judy and Allen Soden, and Robyn and Willy Spizman, and to the memory of Ty Taylor—thank you for reading and responding to our initial drafts and providing us guidance.

We are grateful to the professionals at Gibbs Smith, Publisher who helped us shape our manuscript into its final form. We also appreciate Erica Meyer Rauzin, George Foster and Sue Knopf for their invaluable expertise.

To our children, our parents and our siblings: Brad and Jessica Margolis; Kevin, Michael and Meredith Wilensky; Dorothy and Sol Landau; Renee and Arthur Segan; Candice and Steven Flig; Sheila and Robert Landau; Debbie and Richard Miller; Judy and Adam Segan; Julie and George Stanwick; Donna and Jim Sylvan, as always, we are so grateful for your enduring love, guidance and support.

We are deeply thankful for the constant encouragement that our husbands—Mike and Bob—have provided us. They have been our critics, our counselors and our ongoing source of inspiration. In their own lives, they have been successful in finding and creating workplaces that are true reflections of who they are.

Finally, we are truly indebted to all of our clients. It has been a privilege to help you create workplaces you can call home.

ADDITIONAL RESOURCES

"Drs. Margolis and Wilensky's Five Ps could be rolled into one additional P—Powerful."

Harry Maziar, Retired President & CEO, ZEP Manufacturing Company, and Executive in Residence, Kennesaw State University

There Is No Place Like ♥ Work

Seven Leadership Insights
for Creating a Workplace
to Call Home

Sheila L. Margolis, PhD • Ava S. Wilensky, PhD

Share the insights with others!

For speeches, training and consulting services on
There Is No Place Like Work
and the principles of CORE Culture and the Five Ps
please contact:

CORE InSites® Inc.
5887 Glenridge Drive, Suite 430
Atlanta, GA 30328
404-255-4007
info@coreinsites.com
www.ThereIsNoPlaceLikeWork.com